THE FOOTBALL QUIZ BOOK

THE FOOTBALL QUIZ BOOK

Randy & Warren Etheredge

Hawthorn/Dutton ■ New York

The authors wish to give special thanks to a very special man and athlete who, although we have never met, has taught us how important pride, dignity, courage, and honor are in all things. His retirement is more than just a great loss to football. Thank you, Roger Staubach.

For information contact: Elsevier-Dutton Publishing Co., Inc., 2 Park Avenue, New York, N.Y. 10016

Library of Congress Cataloging in Publication Data

Etheredge, Randy
    The football quiz book.
    1. Football—Miscellanea.   I. Etheredge, Warren, joint author.   II. Title.
GV951.E73   1980   796.332   80-18429

ISBN: 0-8015-2720-1
Published simultaneously in Canada by
Clarke, Irwin & Company Limited, Toronto and Vancouver

Designed by The Etheredges

10 9 8 7 6 5 4 3 2 1

First Edition

The authors gratefully dedicate this book
to each other, without whom
only half of this would have been possible . . .

. . . and, of course, to Mom.

CONTENTS

THE FOOTBALL QUIZ BOOK

KICKOFF

Ever since I can remember, my brother and I have been interested in football. We read anything we can get hold of that is related to football. We collect most any product related to football. And, of course, we watch as many games as we possibly can. I guess we could be considered football addicts. Occasionally during the season our fanaticism gets so bad that schoolwork or some other work assignment goes undone. I suppose that reflects somewhat on our personal priorities, but not badly.

Randy studies the technical aspects of football from the athlete's point of view—in school he played as both a running back and wide receiver. I find I watch at least ten hours a week of football games, review shows, and pregame shows, memorizing the wide range of trivia that fascinates me so—from the names of second-string players to things along the line of the average shoe size of the Steelers front four. Between the two of us we seem to have the game pretty well covered. If you asked the average knowledgeable fan about the longest successful field goal on record, the answer given would probably be: "Tom Dempsey—63 yards—for the Saints in a game against the Eagles." We wouldn't be able to resist adding that Dempsey was not a soccer-style kicker and that his ball holder was Joe Scarpati.

This book was born out of our love and knowledge of professional football and our desire to share our enjoyment in it. We much appreciate the support from our editor, Bob Oskam, in getting this project into play. Now to get you into the game, here is an "opening kickoff" question that should provide you opportunity for an impressive return:

Who are the three players on the cover, and what do they have in common about their Super Bowl MVP awards?

WE'RE #1

There is a first time for everything. How many of these firsts can you identify?

1. Who was the first Heisman Trophy winner to be inducted into the Professional Football Hall of Fame?

2. In 1904 Frank Schiffer, the manager of the Shelby (Ohio) Athletic Club, signed the first black to play pro football. His nickname was the "Black Cyclone." What was his real name?

3. In 1906 an unprecedented event occurred that drastically altered the playing strategy of football. The quarterback of the Canton Bulldogs took the hike from center, dropped back, and *threw* the ball to a teammate downfield. And thus was born the forward pass. Who was football's first receiver?

4. The first NFL president was also among the first to be inducted into Pro Football's Hall of Fame. Who was he?

5. One of the greatest tailback/defensive backs of his time, he played for the Cleveland Bulldogs in 1927, and the Detroit Wolverines in 1928. In 1929 he went to the

New York Giants where he was paid the first big
annual salary ($10,000) of the 1920-32 era. He played
three years for the Giants and then from 1932-34 he
played for the Brooklyn Dodgers.

6. This great halfback/defensive back, as a rookie in 1934,
   became the first member of the 1,000-yard club.

7. The NFL collegiate draft was begun in 1936. The new
   system of selecting college talent for pro ball prevented
   the furious bidding that had gone on for All-Americans
   by giving the first picks to the previous season's losing
   clubs. The team with the worst record in 1935, the
   Philadelphia Eagles (2–9–0) picked first in 1936.
   Philadelphia, however, traded their rights to the
   player they chose to the Chicago Bears. This having
   been done, the athlete promptly announced that he did
   not wish to play pro ball. Who was he?

8. This 5' 6" athlete quarterbacked the Washington Redskins for two years (1952–53) before moving to the
   CFL in 1954. He quickly found Canadian football un-
   suitable and went back to the Redskins in 1955. He
   remained there until 1960 when the newly formed
   Dallas Cowboys traded to get him as their first starting
   quarterback. His lifetime statistics are:

Attempts	Completions	Percentage	Yards
1,796	896	49.94	13,399

TDs	Interceptions
104	141

9. He was the first player ever to gain more than 1,000
   yards via pass receptions in four different seasons:
   1958, 1961, 1962, and 1963.

10. Who was the first player ever selected in an AFL collegiate draft (1959)? Hint: He was a quarterback from Southern Methodist drafted by the Dallas Texans for the 1960 season.

11. Name the first six cities that were supposed to be homes for teams in Lamar Hunt's new American Football League in 1960.

12. Who was the first head coach of the Dallas Cowboys?

13. Who scored the first point in the first Super Bowl (Kansas City Chiefs vs. Green Bay Packers)?

14. Who kicked the first PAT (point-after-touchdown) in the first Super Bowl?

15. The first AFC-NFC Pro Bowl was played in 1971. The NFC won 27 to 6. The offensive and defensive MVPs therefore represented the NFC. Who were they?

16. He was the first Washington Redskin to rush for over 1,000 yards in a single season.

17. In 1973 this pair of running backs from the same backfield became the first to rush for over 1,000 yards apiece in one season.

18. This running back drafted by the Los Angeles Rams in 1977 out of Carthage College is the first athlete from that college to ever be drafted by a professional football team. Who is he?

19. They were the first two NFC pass receivers to each gain over 1,000 yards in the same season on the same team. They accomplished this feat during the 1979 season.

20. The Dallas Cowboys have produced a great many
    champions. One, a defensive tackle became, in 1980,
    the first Cowboy to be inducted into the Pro Football
    Hall of Fame.

21. At the close of the 1931 season, the first All-League
    (All-Pro) team was selected. Who was the player then
    honored as the first string All-League quarterback?

22. Although the original WFL draft is remembered more
    for the "thefts" of Larry Csonka, Calvin Hill, and Jim
    Kiick, the first selection in the draft was, believe it or
    not, a New York Giants running back. Name the Giant
    and the WFL team that selected him.

23. A month before the first WFL draft, a former quarter-
    back for the Bears, Bengals, Bills, and Chargers be-
    came the first NFL/AFL player actually to jump to
    and sign with a WFL team. Who was he?

NICKNAMES

As a general rule, football players find that their names or the names of their teammates do not adequately carry the connotations that the ferocity or quality of their playing ability implies. Hence, many players adopt, or usually have forced upon them, a name that seems to be more appropriate to the image that they and their fans desire. Such is the case with O. J. "The Juice" Simpson. Originally dubbed "Orange Juice" for the O. J. in his name, he eventually became known to his fans as simply "The Juice." Years later, his highly competent offensive line was nicknamed the "Electric Company" because it supplied Simpson with enough "juice" to spring him for his long runs. Although this is actually quite a deviation from the original meaning of his name, it is certainly appropriate.

Below are some of the game's great players, each followed by a selection of four names, any of which very well could be their football aliases—but only one is.

1. Y. A. Tittle
   A. Mr. Title   B. Bald Eagle
   C. Tit Willow   D. Falcon

2. Andy Johnson
   A. Apple Juice   B. Grapefruit Juice
   C. A. Jay Johnson, Jr.   D. LadyBird

3. R. C. Owens
   A. Cola Bear
   C. Alley-Oop
   B. Butterfingers
   D. Racey

4. Elroy Hirsch
   A. Crazy Legs
   C. Magic
   B. Hirschy Boy
   D. Royel

5. Randy White
   A. Too Tough
   C. Terrorist
   B. Monster
   D. Manster

6. Ted Hendricks
   A. Sticks
   C. Stork
   B. Stoned
   D. Night Stalker

7. Dallas's Defense
   A. Sack Pack
   C. Gold Rush
   B. Silver Rush
   D. Doomsday

8. Rich Saul
   A. Dr. Kildare
   C. Malpractice
   B. General Hospital
   D. Doctor's Hospital

9. San Francisco's Defense
   A. Sack Pack
   C. Gold Rush
   B. Silver Rush
   D. Doomsday

10. Cliff Harris
    A. Masher
    C. Killer
    B. Crash
    D. Assassin

11. Baltimore's Defense
    A. Sack Pack
    C. Gold Rush
    B. Silver Rush
    D. Doomsday

12. Jack Reynolds
    A. Hammer
    C. Jigsaw
    B. Circular Saw
    D. Hacksaw

13. Walter Payton
    A. Sweet
    C. Dynamite
    B. Dynamo
    D. Sweetness

14. Eddie Payton
    A. Sweet
    C. Dynamite
    B. Payton Place
    D. Sweetness

15. Monte Johnson
    A. Shadow
    C. Batman
    B. Phantom
    D. The Spirit

16. Thomas Henderson
    A. Beverly Hills
    C. Hollywood
    B. Superstar
    D. Broadway

17. Fred Williamson
    A. Hammer
    C. The Drill
    B. Hacksaw
    D. Nail

18. Norm Van Brocklin
    A. The Norwegian
    C. The Frenchman
    B. The Dutchman
    D. The Belgian

19. L. G. Dupre
    A. Goodbye
    C. Long Gone
    B. Elgie
    D. Streaker

20. Clyde Turner
    A. Bulldog
    C. Doberman
    B. Maddog
    D. Kitty Cat

21. Skip Thomas
    A. Dr. Doom   B. Sir
    C. DOA   D. Dr. Death

22. Joe Lavender
    A. Oscar   B. Big Bird
    C. Kermit   D. Stork

23. Ron Jaworski
    A. Polish Shotgun   B. Polish Pistol
    C. Polish Slingshot   D. Polish Rifle

24. Billy "White Shoes" Johnson
    A. Tickets   B. Grand Stand
    C. Box Office   D. Showcase

25. Ray Hamilton
    A. Sugar Bear   B. Honey Bear
    C. Cola Bear   D. Teddy Bear

MUDDLE IN THE HUDDLE #1 (CENTERS)

This is the first of three quizzes in which the names of ten exceptional athletes who have set standards of playing quality in relatively glamourless positions have been encoded.

Each letter below corresponds to another; for example *z* might stand for *h*, and *g* for *q*, etc.

To help you get started the players' years and teams are listed below their anagrams.

All the players here are or were centers.

1. PWV SWBFARKXU
Philadelphia Eagles, 1963. Pittsburgh Steelers, 1964–76.

2. CRS IYYI
Oakland Raiders, 1960–74.

3. JKB GIHSWB
Green Bay Packers, 1964–73.

4. CIZB ARYLQKPWXU
Dallas Cowboys, 1971–   .

5. MWPX SWEMJ
   Baltimore Colts, 1969. Miami Dolphins, 1970. San
   Diego Chargers, 1971–74. Houston Oilers, 1975– .

6. QKIPQK JWPFYKBF
   Detroit Lions, 1949.

7. SKX ZKRB
   (also played LB); New York Giants, 1931–45. Head
   coach of the Los Angeles Dons in 1947.

8. CKAA NWB BIYK
   Atlanta Falcons, 1969– .

9. URMJ FLVSWBFJR
   Baltimore Colts, 1955–68.

10. PRMZ FWEX
    Los Angeles Rams, 1970– .

HOME-FIELD ADVANTAGE

The home-field advantage has been figured into bettors' handicaps since football began. Its relevance has been hotly disputed for just as long. "Any team can beat any other, anywhere, on any given Sunday." Nevertheless, whether it be a "dust bowl," "ice bowl," or "Superdome," many fans and players become emotionally attached to their particular stadium, raising its importance well above just a field to play on.

Each question here is a set of two clues. First, with only one clue try to guess the identity of the stadium and the team that plays there. If you can't, the second clue should give it away.

1a. Home of the "Tyler Rose."

2a. Built on the site of the 1964 World's Fair.

3a. Foxboro.

4a. "Unfinished Stadium."

5a. Site of 1979–80 Pro Bowl.

6a. Where they came marching in.

7a. The architects are Naramore, Skilling, and Praeger.

8a. Site of five Super Bowls.

9a. "In the swamps."

10a. Auto racetrack.

11a. Home team shares the same sideline with the visitors.

12a. "Electric Company"

13a. Final *playing field* of "The Juice."

14a. Joe Brown's bronze statues stand outside.

15a. Just "over the hill."

16a. Present home of the Dallas Texans.

17a. 1,760 yards.

18a. Paul Brown's second.

19a. Four out of four Super Bowls.

20a. Bill Walsh.

21a. The beer baron.

22a. Built primarily for the Athletics.

23a. In 1967: 46,500. In 1976: 71,000.

24a. Inflatable roof.

25a. The most expensive stadium ever built in America. Estimated cost, $63 million.

26a. A previous, and possible future, site of the Olympics.

27a. Ex-home of the Titans.

28a. Packers

1b. The first dome.

2b. Queens.

3b. Located between Boston and Providence.

4b. Irving.

5b. Site of 1980–81 Pro Bowl.

6b. Site of Super Bowl IX.

7b. The most recently built dome.

8b. Home of the only team to go undefeated in an entire season.

9b. New Jersey.

10b. Adorned with colonnade.

11b. Site of the famous "Hail Mary Pass," (1975–76).

12b. First home of "The Juice."

13b. Home of the Philadelphia bartender-turned-kicker.

14b. Spectrum's neighbor.

15b. Originally called D.C. Stadium.

16b. Lamar Hunt's.

17b. Orange Crush.

18b. On the Ohio.

19b. Home of the "Terrible Towel."

20b. Play by the bay.

21b. Under the Arch.

22b. Al Davis.

23b. Southern expansion.

24b. Pontiac.

25b. The Saints come marching in.

26b. Ex-home of the Rams.

27b. Ex-home of the Giants.

28b. Not Milwaukee County Stadium.

PLAYER IDENTIFICATIONS

To answer the one hundred questions that follow, one merely proceeds as the title implies: identify the player(s) using the given clues. The difficulty involved ranges from relatively easy to not so easy to "you probably won't have any idea." The three sections are: First and Ten (the easiest); Second and Eight (more difficult); and Third and Thirteen (the hardest). Wherever questions indicate a present position, that is as of the closing of the 1979 season.

FIRST AND TEN

1. "The world's fastest human" played wide receiver for the Dallas Cowboys.

2. He has been playing for the Cleveland Browns since 1970 as a defensive tackle. His playing ability is so proficient that he was once voted the best defensive lineman by his peers. He is certainly one of the lesser known "defensive greats."

3. While attending Penn State this Steeler thousand-yard rusher almost played second fiddle to another Nittany Lion running back named Lydell Mitchell.

4. Toward the end of his career, this football star was more of a personality than a player. He was born in Beaver Falls, but became famous in a more cosmopolitan area.

5. Although he has anchored the St. Louis Cardinal offensive front since 1974, he has been generally overlooked because of his All-Pro linemate (tackle, Dan Dierdorf). He joined the team in 1971.

6. He has been a kicker for the Philadelphia Eagles (1970) and the Houston Oilers (1971–72). He is now the starting kicker for the Washington Redskins (1974–   ). In 1979, he was second only to John Smith (New England Patriots, 115 points) in total points scored with 114.

7. In 1979, the Tampa Bay Buccaneers' starting quarterback was drafted out of Grambling College.

8. When veteran quarterback Jim Plunkett separated his shoulder for a second time, in 1975, this rookie became the head of the Patriot offensive attack.

9. In his day he was one of the great offensive guards in pro ball.
   Kansas City Chief fans were saddened when his fourteen-year career ended in 1976. On the bright side, his son, also an offensive lineman, was drafted in the first round by the Chiefs in 1980. Name the father and son changing the guard.

10. This Penn State graduate received "Rookie of the Year" honors for his performances in the NASL (North American Soccer League) during the summer of 1976. Later that fall he started as kicker for the Cincinnati Bengals.

11. The brother of the above-mentioned athlete is now the starting kicker for the Pittsburgh Steelers.

12. He became the Minnesota Vikings' starting quarterback after Fran Tarkenton retired.

13. The promising career of this Patriot wide receiver was ended by a vicious Jack "The Assassin" Tatum tackle.

14. This legend was the Oakland Raider kicker and a back-up quarterback before he was forced to resign at the age of forty-nine. He was replaced by rookie Fred Steinfort who was younger and "more suited for the job." (Fred Steinfort was traded at the end of his first season for being ineffective.)

15. Before the 1979 season the Miami Dolphins tried to balance out their offense and take some of the pressure off their receivers by acquiring this running back from San Francisco.

16. The O.J. running back of the St. Louis Cardinals.

17. Once upon a time (1974–75), he was the starting quarterback for the Los Angeles Rams. He is now a back-up for Dan Fouts at San Diego. In 1974, he won the Pro Bowl MVP award.

18. Like Billy "White Shoes" Johnson of the Oilers, this Denver Bronco wide receiver has become more famous for his dazzling kick returns than for his actual performances as a talented receiver.

19. During most of Mike McCormack's era as the coach of the Philadelphia Eagles, a critical flaw existed in their offense. They almost completely lacked a running attack. For instance, in 1975 (they finished 4 and 10) they

managed to gain only 1,072 total yards on the ground.

In 1977, Dick Vermeil, who had taken over the Eagles' coaching job in 1976, quickly remedied the problem by drafting his running back from Abilene Christian. The statistics for 1978 show him fifth in the NFL with 1,220 yards on 259 carries for a 4.2-yard average and 11 touchdowns. After the 1979 season he moved up to fourth place in the league with 1,512 yards on 338 carries for a 4.5-yard average and 9 touchdowns. He had rushed 340 more yards in 1979 than the entire team did in 1975.

20. Although it is not obvious in his game performances, this Jet receiver is legally blind in one eye.

21. This Pittsburgh Steeler is famous for his seemingly "psychopathic" tendencies while playing linebacker.

22. Though bothered by injuries and inept performances by some of his teammates, this defensive tackle has remained (since 1972) the stalwart of the Giants' defensive line and one of the star performers in any Giant game.

23. Although he did not start until the tenth game of the 1977 season, this collegiate superstar still managed to gain 1,007 yards for the Dallas Cowboys.

24. This versatile Minnesota running back (1973–79) caught 73 passes in 1975, setting an NFL record in the process. Recently, though, he was traded to New England.

25. One of the most tragic moments of the 1979 season occurred during a pre-season workout when this starting St. Louis Cardinal tight end mysteriously died

after running a regular pass pattern. (Doctors never discovered the cause of death.)

Since 1960, the team's first year of existence, the Oakland Raiders have had many quarterbacks and coaches but only two starting centers.

26. From 1960–74 the Raider center was quite an individualist from his playing style to his double zero uniform number.

27. The succeeding center, still playing, is a little more subtle about his uniqueness but he is certainly worthy of his All-Star companions.

28. A key to the revitalized offense which led the Los Angeles Rams to Super Bowl XIV was the blossoming of this little (5'10", 188 lb.) running back.

29. Along with Cliff Harris of the Cowboys, this Washington Redskin was a consistent All-NFC safety.

30. Dallas fans like to call the Seattle Seahawks the "Second String Cowboys," while Seattle's fans humorously claim the Cowboys to be the "Seahawks' Farm Club." Whatever the case may be, there certainty is a startling percentage of ex-Cowboys on the Seahawks' roster. Undoubtedly one of the most significant refugees is a left-handed quarterback who Tom Landry axed at the final cut-point before the 1976 season. He has gone on to become a brilliant starter, displaying great potential for the Seahawks.

31. After an exhibition fight with Muhammad Ali, this Denver Bronco defensive lineman suggested that he might follow a career in boxing. Instead, he got himself traded to the Cleveland Browns.

32. This St. Louis Cardinal wide receiver is also a 9.2 (hundred yard) sprinter who has terrified opposing defensive backs since 1972.

33. As insurance for the recently injury-prone Ken Anderson, the Cincinnati Bengals made their first pick in the 1979 collegiate draft this athlete from Washington State, nicknamed the "Throwin' Samoan."

34. In his first year (1970) it seemed as if Pittsburgh's high draft choice had been wasted on this quarterback from Louisiana Tech. But as he matured he led the Steelers to becoming one of football's finest teams.

35. Due to a critical injury, Pat Haden (quarterback) had to relinquish the reins of the Rams to this player.

36. To strengthen their line-up of quarterbacks the Denver Broncos acquired this mustached, one-time starter from the Jets during the 1979 post-season.

37. He is not the greatest running back in NFL history, but he is a very reliable and very underrated rusher who has been with the Giants since 1974.

38. He was a quarterback for the 49ers (1961–66), the Saints (1967–70), and, most notably, for the Redskins (1971–78). He completed 1,562 out of 2,939 passes (53.14%) for 20,179 yards. He threw 143 interceptions and 148 TDs.

39. Temperamental Cardinal guard turned Saint.

40. He won the Heisman trophy as a sophomore quarterback in 1963. He was selected as a future choice in the tenth round of the 1964 NFL draft. He joined the pros in 1969 after four years of military service. In 1971–72

he led his team to win their first Super Bowl. He did it again in 1977–78. His lifetime statistics are simply, honestly, phenomenal. He is considered by many to be the greatest quarterback that ever played. He retired in 1979.

SECOND AND EIGHT

1. He is called the "last of the Sixty-Minute Men." When he played for the Eagles from 1949 through 1962 he was both a center and a linebacker.

2. This All-Pro tackle for the Atlanta Falcons was traded to the Baltimore Colts after the 1975 season for the draft rights to Steve Bartkowski. He retired after 1978.

3. During Tampa Bay's first year (1976) he was both their punter and placekicker.

4. This defensive tackle from UCLA was the Seattle Seahawks' first selection in the 1979 collegiate draft. It is said that he hits as hard as his name is to pronounce.

5. A severe rodeo injury forced this Dallas Cowboy running back into retirement. He played from 1966 to 1974. In that time he gained 3,886 yards on 899 carries.

6. This quarterback holds a top-ten position in almost every lifetime passing category. He played for the Washington Redskins (1961–63), the Philadelphia Eagles (1964–70), the Minnesota Vikings (1971), the New York Giants (1972–74), the San Francisco 49ers (1974–75), and the New York Giants (1976).

7. This spunky defensive back came from the CFL to aid the Houston Oilers in their quest for the 1979 NFL Championship. The Oilers did not make it to Super Bowl XIV but his inspired play with several interceptions in the playoff game against the San Diego Chargers made him a true "big play" man and a person to watch in 1980.

8. A major disruption came to the NFL's "powers that be" with the new-found prominence of the NFL Players Association. Who is the executive director of this organization?

9. During his career with the Los Angeles Rams (1961–71), the San Diego Chargers (1972–73), and the Washington Redskins (1974), this defensive end put true fear into the hearts of opposing players. His real name is David but he's more commonly known by his "ministerial" nickname.

10. When he ended his nine-year career with the Cleveland Browns in 1966 he had rushed for 12,312 yards. Only once did he not exceed 1,000 yards; in 1962 he only gained 996 yards.

11. In 1963 two outstanding players were suspended by Bert Bell (the NFL Commissioner) for their involvement in illegal gambling. It was a definite blotch on the careers of a defensive end for the Detroit Lions (1958–70) and the "Golden Boy from Notre-Dame," a running back for the Green Bay Packers (1957–66).

12. These two safeties have been playing together in the Chicago Bears' defensive backfield since 1976. This Ohio State grad and this Yale grad have become notorious for their devastating, but clean, tackles.

13. He quarterbacked the Kansas City Chiefs after Len Dawson and before Steve Fuller.

14. The two starting running backs for the New Orleans Saints are very appropriately called "Thunder and Lightning." Their combined stats for 1979 are awesome, to say the least: 1,906 yards gained on the ground with 98 receptions for an additional 729 yards. They both joined the team in 1976.

15. A fullback for the Buffalo Bills from 1971 until he was traded in 1978 was almost completely overlooked because of the consistently outstanding performances of his running mate O. J. Simpson.

16. This defensive end for the Minnesota Vikings (1961–79) holds the record for playing in the most consecutive games. He is also humorously remembered for his 70-yard fumble return for a touchdown . . . unfortunately he ran in the wrong direction and scored for the other team.

17. From 1956–67 this Baltimore Colt running back provided many explosive moments. His stats speak for themselves:

As a running back:	Carries	Yards	Average	TDs
	1,069	5,174	4.84	63

As a flanker:	Receptions	Yards	Average	TDs
	363	6,039	16.64	48

18. Since the 1976 season this athlete has been playing defensive tackle for the New York Jets. In his rookie year he was known by the more common name of Larry Faulk.

19. Even though one of the finest tight ends ever to play the game, he unfortunately will be remembered for a reception he didn't make for the Dallas Cowboys in Super Bowl XIII.

20. During the 1979 season this 6'8" Philadelphia Eagle wide receiver set the record for the most consecutive games with at least one reception.

21. Whose record did the answer-to-the-preceding-question shatter? He was a wide receiver for the New Orleans Saints (1967–73) and the Buffalo Bills (1975).

22. The Los Angeles Rams' offensive line was dealt a serious blow when this veteran from 1966 retired after the 1978 season. His departure left a big gap in the guard position.

23. Many football experts are now saying that one possible explanation for the Detroit Lions not having made it to the 1979 playoffs as had been widely predicted was the loss of this quarterback from Purdue due to injury. He started with the Lions in 1976. (In 1974 and 1975 he played for the New York Stars, the Charlotte Hornets, and the Chicago Fire of the WFL).

24. He was a quarterback for both the Los Angeles Rams (1949–57) and the Philadelphia Eagles (1958–60). After retiring he became a head coach for the Minnesota Vikings (1961–66) and the Atlanta Falcons (1968–74).

25. Year after year this Giant punter is one of the top five punters in the league. In the 1979 season he was ranked second with 104 punts for 4,445 yards and a 42.7 average.

26. Who was ranked first in 1979? He punted 89 times for 3,883 yards and a 43.6-yard average. He plays for the Kansas City Chiefs.

27. Going into the 1979 season Cincinnati Bengals fans' hopes were high because of their new defensive front four. It was dubbed "WEBB." Each letter in the nickname is a last initial of one of the linemen.

28. From 1955–67 he was a superb pass catcher for the Baltimore Colts. Now he's coaching the same team's receivers.

29. He was considered the best Tampa Bay Buccaneer defenseman before the 1979 season. But to the surprise of football prophets and prognosticators he was soon traded to the Oakland Raiders.

30. Just prior to the 1979 season, Don Shula had to decide who would be the starting kicker for the Miami Dolphins. The choice was between a twelve-year veteran and a seventh-round draft pick from Oklahoma. The incumbent was beaten. Name both the veteran and the rookie.

31. Although their first-round draft choice, Tom Cousineau, defected to the CFL, the Buffalo Bills managed to better their 5-and-11 1978 record in 1979 with a 7-and-9 record because of a fine group of rookies. A good example of this fresh talent is the Bills' #1b-picked wide receiver from Clemson.

32. He used to be the starting quarterback of the New York Giants' "prevent offense," but between the 1979 and 1980 seasons he was traded to the Philadelphia Eagles.

33. In 1972 he was known as Bobby Moore; he is no longer. He is a wide receiver who played for the St. Louis Cardinals (1972–73), the Buffalo Bills (1974–75), and has been playing for the Minnesota Vikings since 1976. What is his name?

34. For more than half the year that the Miami Dolphins had a perfect season (1972) the regular quarterback, Bob Griese, sat on the bench nursing a broken leg. Who guided the Dolphins for most of that season?

35. This "speedy" Cleveland Brown kick returner took over the starting fullback role after the legendary Jim Brown retired to follow a career in the movies.

36. In 1978 this All-American tight end was drafted in the first round out of Notre Dame by the San Francisco 49ers. His 1979 statistics show him to be a strong second-year performer with good potential: 24 receptions, 266 yards, 11.1-yard average, and 3 touchdowns.

37. At first, the trade of Baltimore Colt running back, Lydell Mitchell, to the San Diego Chargers for this all-purpose back was unpopular. However, due to several injuries to Bert Jones, this ex-Charger became one of the only highlights of the 1978 and 1979 Colt seasons.

38. For years he has been the anchor of the Miami Dolphins' strong offensive line. After the 1979 season he was considering retirement if not traded.

39. The Tampa Bay Buccaneers waited until the closing minutes of the 1979 regular season to clinch a playoff spot. The final score of their sixteenth game (against the Kansas City Chiefs) came in the last quarter. It was a 19-yard field goal which won it 3–0 and sent the

Buccaneers to the playoffs. Who was the Tampa Bay kicker?

40. He began his career as a running back/kick returner for the Baltimore Colts (1967–69) and as such participated in Super Bowl III against the New York Jets: he returned two kickoffs for 59 yards. In 1970 he moved to the Pittsburgh Steelers. He played in their Super Bowl IX against the Minnesota Vikings: he returned one kickoff for 15 yards. In 1975, the Dallas Cowboys picked him up on waivers and put him in their starting halfback position. He performed admirably, developing the reputation of being the one to get the yardage on third and long. With the acquisition of Heisman Trophy winner Tony Dorsett, he lost his starting spot but Tom Landry still considers him a "starter" because of his third down activity. As a matter of fact, in 1978 he led the team in receptions with 47. His appearances in Dallas' Super Bowls X, XII, and XIII added to those at Baltimore and Pittsburgh tie him for the record for participating in five Super Bowls.

THIRD AND THIRTEEN

1. In 1971 the New England Patriots signed a 5′10″ wide receiver/defensive back from Stanford to run under the passes of the veteran Jim Plunkett. (An interesting footnote is that when he was younger, because of his size, he was employed as one of Disneyland's Seven Dwarves.)

2. When Earl Campbell rushed for 1,450 yards in his rookie season (1978) he broke this San Diego Charger running back's record. (Most yards gained in a rookie season.)

3. Although he carried the ball 94 times for 525 yards (an astonishing 5.6-yard average) and 5 touchdowns in 1973, this was not enough to keep his Chicago Bear fans from booing him. Not that Chicago fans are hard to please, it's just that this player was a quarterback not a running back. Finally, coach Abe Gibron was persuaded to start rookie Gary Huff. Huff, unfortunately, was no improvement and this quarterback returned to the starting position. Yet the fans kept booing . . . Perhaps this was because along with his 5.6-yard rushing average he only completed 47 percent of his passes.

4. This Hall-of-Famer was a defensive back for the St. Louis Cardinals (1960–72) who made famous the safety blitz. At the closing of the 1979 season he was hired as intermediate coach for his former team.

5. This free agent out of Kansas State came to the Green Bay Packers in 1978 and didn't catch a single pass. But 1979 proved to be a bit of an improvement. He became the team's leading receiver with 56 receptions, 711 yards, and 4 touchdowns. Amazingly, he is a tight end, not a wide receiver.

6. According to Vince Lombardi, he was the best cornerback to ever play the game of football. From 1952 through 1965 he intercepted 68 passes; and in 1954 he set the record for most interceptions in a single season with 14. He played for the Los Angeles Rams (1952–53), the Chicago Cardinals (1954–59), and the Detroit Lions (1960–65).

7. Before the Atlanta Falcons developed the "Grits Blitz," he was, perhaps, the only "star" the team ever had. Surprisingly, he was a linebacker not an offensive player. He played from 1966 through 1976.

8. The 1974 season was the first in nine years that the Dallas Cowboys failed to reach the NFC playoffs. Even so, the team provided many a thrilling moment during the regular season. The traditional Thanksgiving Day game versus the Washington Redskins is a good example. Coming off the bench to replace the injured Roger Staubach, this rookie led Dallas to a 24–23 comeback victory via a 50-yard bomb to Drew Pearson with only 28 seconds left in the game.

9. The Dallas Texans employed one of the most spectacular kick returners of the 1962 season (the year they won the AFL Championship). He returned 18 kickoffs for 535 yards and a 29.7-yard average. He played for the Texans (1961–62), the Chiefs (the Texans renamed) from 1963–64, and then the Oakland Raiders (1965–70).

10. A key to the success of Marv Levy's Wing-T formation at Kansas City has been the steady performance of this eleven-year veteran at center.

11. Although they only won six games in the 1970 season, the Chicago Bears did find something to be happy about: this player tied an NFL record by returning four season kickoffs for touchdowns.

12. Pete Rozelle's predecessor as the NFL commissioner died in 1960 of a heart attack while watching a game between the Philadelphia Eagles (a team that he coached, 1938–40) and the Pittsburgh Steelers (a team that he coached in 1941 and co-owned with Art Rooney) on the University of Pennsylvania Franklin Field where he had played college football. Who was he?

13. The 1975 season was a particularly dreary one for the Atlanta Falcons. Their 4–10 won/loss record did not

provide much excitement. Yet there was one highlight: a running back gained 1,002 yards on 250 carries and scored 5 touchdowns. Who is he?

14. One of the most outstanding guards ever was a Cleveland Brown who played from 1946 through 1953. His achievements were finally acknowledged with his induction into the Hall of Fame in 1977.

15. The second best college punter of 1975 (Tulsa State) came to the NFL with a 46.6-yard average. He was the first starting punter for the Seattle Seahawks. In 1976 he punted 80 times but his average dropped to 38.3.

16. One of the major components in the Cincinnati Bengals drive to the 1970 playoffs, while starting quarterback Greg Cook was sidelined (Virgil Carter replaced him), was the consistent kicking of this second-year veteran. He played for the Bengals (1969–74) and the Philadelphia Eagles (1975–77). In 1970 he connected on 33 out of 33 extra-point tries and kicked 25 out of 37 field goals.

17. In 1965 this Chicago Bear running back gained 867 yards rushing, a 5.2-yard average, and 14 touchdowns. He also gained 507 yards receiving with 6 touchdowns; and 898 yards returning punts and kickoffs while addling 2 more touchdowns. And to top off his All-Pro rookie season he also completed 2 out of 3 passes for 53 yards and another touchdown. His 22 touchdowns that year set an NFL record for the most scored by a single athlete in a single season. His stats continued to surpass those of most others during the 1966 and 1967 seasons. The 1968 season reaped 856 yards rushing, but in what was then called the "crack heard around the world" a hit made by a San Francisco 49ers defensive back ripped the ligament and cartilage in his right

knee. He recovered. He recovered enough to become the league-leading rusher in 1969 with 1,032 yards and a 4.7-yard average. Unfortunately, in 1970 he reinjured his knee and had to undergo surgery. This injury was his downfall. During 1970 and 1971 he rushed for a total of only 90 yards. After the 1971 season, this "superstar" in the truest sense had played football for the last time.

18. Name the San Francisco 49er defensive back who hit the subject of the above question in 1968, inadvertently breaking his knee.

19. After Bart Starr retired in 1971, this quarterback started for the Green Bay Packers until the end of 1973. In 1974 he was the back-up quarterback for Buffalo. Then he moved to Atlanta in 1976, to become their back-up quarterback.

20. He was the middle linebacker for the Chicago Cardinals in 1957. He remained there until he was traded in 1958 to San Francisco. Two good seasons were spent with the 49ers and then in 1960 when the Dallas Cowboys joined the league he began a tradition of greatness in his position by becoming their first middle linebacker.

NAME FIND (COACHES)

Find the last names of these Head Coaches hidden in the puzzle.

1. George ALLEN
2. Paul BROWN
3. Monte CLARK
4. Dan DEVINE
5. Weeb EWBANK
6. Abe GIBRON
7. Bud GRANT
8. Forrest GREGG
9. George HALAS
10. Lou HOLTZ
11. Pop IVY
12. Chuck KNOX
13. Tom LANDRY
14. Vince LOMBARDI

15. Marv LEVY
16. John MADDEN
17. Ted MARCHIBRODA
18. "Red" MILLER
19. "Greasy" NEALE
20. Chuck NOLL
21. Steve OWEN
22. Jack PARDEE
23. Homer RICE
24. Lou SABAN
25. Bart STARR
26. Hank STRAM
27. Bill WALSH
28. Paul WIGGIN

N	A	B	A	S	Y	K	N	A	B	W	E
E	Z	O	T	R	V	V	H	C	E	L	I
P	A	R	D	E	E	S	I	X	N	H	S
K	A	N	C	N	L	N	E	W	O	A	S
M	A	I	I	A	O	N	O	L	L	N	T
L	R	V	W	E	M	R	T	A	T	N	K
N	E	L	L	A	B	Z	H	I	A	O	R
D	B	A	C	L	A	R	K	R	S	R	E
R	E	P	T	G	R	E	G	G	A	B	L
N	O	M	A	D	D	E	N	T	P	I	L
A	W	I	G	G	I	N	S	E	L	G	I
T	A	D	O	R	B	I	H	C	R	A	M

MUDDLE IN THE HUDDLE #2 (DEFENSIVE LINEMEN)

A new code, a new collection of well-known and less-known athletes in anagram form. They all are or were defensive lineman. The usual information is included—their dates and teams.

1. VAWT TARWA
   New York Giants, 1969–71. Los Angeles Rams, 1972–   .

2. MBM CSCCR
   Dallas Cowboys, 1961–74.

3. TWFPBJ KBJWU
   Los Angeles Rams, 1961–71. San Diego Chargers, 1972–73. Washington Redskins, 1974.

4. "DWFJ" KBW NAWWJW
   Pittsburgh Steelers, 1969–   .

5. CBHSW LWCPZWA
   San Diego Chargers, 1975–   .

6. UXWGW JSWZFHU
   Seattle Seahawks, 1976–78. Minnesota Vikings,
   1979– .

7. FJTR ABMHUXWCCS
   Los Angeles Rams, 1951–55. New York Giants,
   1956–64.

8. CWABR UWCDBJ
   Tampa Bay Buccaneers, 1976–   .

9. NSJB DFAPZWXXS
   Dallas Texans, 1952. Baltimore Colts, 1953–66.

10. WAJSW UXFHXJWA
    Pittsburgh Steelers, 1950–63.

RAINBOWS TO SIX

The bomb: the long-arching, spiraling pass is perhaps the most loved and feared play in all of football. Few quarterbacks dare to risk it; some fear interceptions, others aren't confident in their receivers. Yet, fortunately there is a small and elite group of football's finest that has become reknown for the amazing ability to build rainbows to the end zone.

Listed below are some of these great quarterbacks. Match them with their equally famous receivers.

1. Johnny Unitas   A. Don Maynard

2. Roger Staubach   B. Boyd Dowler

3. Fran Tarkenton   C. Hugh McElhenny

4. Bart Starr   D. Steve Largent

5. Len Dawson   E. Ernest Gray

6. Terry Bradshaw   F. Sammie White

7. Sonny Jurgensen   G. Ken Burrough

8. Ken Stabler	H. Lance Alworth
9. Joe Namath	I. Jimmy Orr
10. Ken Anderson	J. Drew Pearson
11. John Hadl	K. Elroy Hirsch
12. Norm Van Brocklin	L. Fred Biletnikoff
13. Dan Fouts	M. Pete Retzlaff
14. Craig Morton	N. Haven Moses
15. Phil Simms	O. Issac Curtis
16. Bob Griese	P. Dante Lavelli and Mac Speedie
17. Dan Pastorini	Q. Paul Warfield
18. Otto Graham	R. John Jefferson
19. Y. A. Tittle	S. Lynn Swann
20. Jim Zorn	T. Otis Taylor

NAME FIND (LINEBACKERS)

Find the last names of these linebackers hidden in the puzzle.

1. Bobby BELL

2. Bill BERGEY

3. Robert BRAZILLE

4. Doug BUFFONE

5. Nick BUONICONTI

6. Dick BUTKUS

7. Fred CARR

8. Harry CARSON

9. Mike CURTIS

10. Brad DUSEK

11. Chris HANBURGER

12. Tommy HART

13. Thomas HENDERSON

14. Chuck HOWLEY

15. Lee Roy JORDAN

16. Willie LANIER

17. Jim LECLAIR

18. D. D. LEWIS

19. Mike LUCCI

20. Paul NAUMOFF

21. Tommy NOBIS

22. Andy RUSSEL

23. Jeff SIEMON

24. Stan WHITE

```
H  S  N  R  U  S  S  E  L  L  E  B

K  E  S  U  D  Y  E  G  R  E  B  U

H  A  N  B  U  R  G  E  R  W  B  O

K  A  J  D  I  C  U  R  T  I  S  N

C  D  R  C  E  T  I  H  W  S  N  I

B  H  C  T  A  R  N  O  B  I  S  C

R  U  D  C  A  R  S  O  N  E  U  O

L  R  F  N  A  D  R  O  J  M  K  N

S  I  F  F  O  M  U  A  N  O  T  T

Y  E  L  W  O  H  U  U  M  N  U  I

D  L  R  E  I  N  A  L  E  L  B  Y

B  R  A  Z  I  L  E  C  L  A  I  R
```

SCRIMMAGED LINES

The names that follow are all of professional players who have held the position of tight end. Each name has its correct place in the blank crossword diagram on the facing page. Put each player "on-sides" in the corect position in this diagram.

4-LETTER NAMES
Don BASS
Reuben GANT
J. V. CAIN
John David CROW

5-LETTER NAMES
Jimmie GILES
Riley ODOMS
Charles YOUNG
Bruce HARDY
Jackie SMITH
Greg LATTA

6-LETTER NAMES
Billy Joe DUPREE
Dave CASPER
Henry CHILDS
Bob TUCKER
Jean FUGETT
Mike BARBER
Jerome BARKUM

7-LETTER NAMES
Paul COFFMAN
Russ FRANCIS
Raymond CHESTER
Keith KREPFLE

8-LETTER NAME
Jim MITCHELL

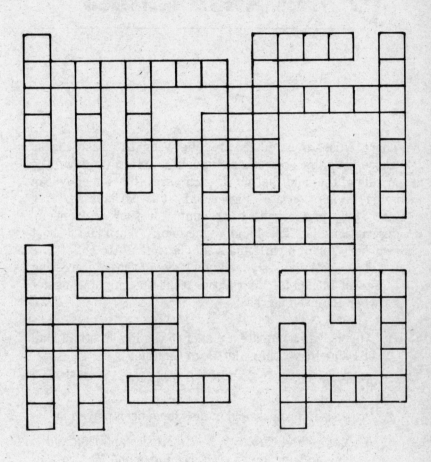

BETWEEN THE HASH MARKS

There exists a nebulous area between the hash marks (those little lines on either side and in two rows down the middle of the field that mark each yard) that somehow can never be appropriately described. It is perhaps the only inaccuracy of football. It accounts for such announcers' descriptions as: "Third and a long one," "Third and a short two," or "About a yard and a coupla footballs to go."

This section tests your knowledge of those interesting tidbits of incidental information that one might consider between the hash marks.

1. Anyone can nominate a player to the Pro Football Hall of Fame by writing a letter to Canton.

   A. True   B. False

2. Pre-season professional games have been played in

   A. Mexico and Cuba   B. Mexico and England
   C. England and Japan   D. Japan and Mexico

3. The annual award for "Outstanding Contribution to Professional Football and the Community" is called the

   A. Joe Namath Award   B. Johnny Unitas Award
   C. Sammy Baugh Award   D. Paul Hornung Award

4. Randall's Island's Downing Stadium has housed, at one time or another a great many pro teams: the New York Cosmos (NASL), the New York Stars (WFL), the New York Fillies (Women's Football League), and what pro (men's) football team?

A. Brooklyn Dodgers
B. New York Giants
C. New York Yankees
D. New York Titans

5. In 1923 a franchise was granted to the Frankford Yellow Jackets. Today they are known as the

A. Kansas City Chiefs
B. Green Bay Packers
C. Pittsburgh Steelers
D. Cleveland Browns

6. The annual award for "Excellence On and Off the Playing Field" is called the

A. NFL Citizenship Award
B. Byron R. "Whizzer" White Award
C. Johnny Unitas Award
D. NFL Outstanding Contribution Award

7. Is it legal for the eligible receivers of a team to wear helmets of a different color than those of their teammates provided that the receivers' helmets are all of a uniform color?

A. Yes
B. No

8. The coldest game ever played was the 1967 Championship. The temperature during the "Ice Bowl" dropped to −13°F. Which two teams participated in that game?

A. Dallas and Green Bay
B. Minnesota and New York
C. New York and Chicago
D. Dallas and Minnesota

9. The hottest game ever played took place between the Miami Dolphins and the San Francisco 49ers in the Orange Bowl in 1973. The temperature reached

A. 99°   B. 110°
C. 115°   D. 125°

10. A professional football must weigh between

A. 12–13 oz.   B. 13–14 oz.
C. 14–15 oz.   D. 15–16 oz.

11. The tallest player on record was a Kansas City Chief tight end at 6′10″. What is his name?

A. Ed Jones   B. Morris Stroud
C. Ed Podolak   D. Deacon Jones

12. During the 1950s, when innovative facemasks were the rage, clear Lucite was experimented with. It had its advantages. It could be molded into any shape, it was very hard and could be seen through. However, after only a short time of usage, the Lucite facemask was outlawed because of its one drawback: It often broke or shattered, gashing both tacklers and ball carriers.

A. True   B. False

13. A professional football must be inflated to how many pounds of pressure?

A. 12   B. 13
C. 14   D. 15

14. An astronaut experiences approximately 6–10 Gs of pressure at takeoff. A jet pilot often passes out at 20 Gs. Dr. Stephen Ried tested the G force of a tackle

made by a Detroit Lions' linebacker, Joe Schmidt, during the 1962 Pro Bowl. He found the force of one tackle to be equivalent to

A. 10 Gs.   B. 30 Gs.
C. 50 Gs.   D. 60 Gs.

15. The heaviest player on record played for the Detroit Lions from 1948 through 1954. He weighed 349½ pounds. Who was he?

A. Les Bingaman   B. Alex Karras
C. Leon Hart   D. Lou Creekmur

16. During a game on third and long a linebacker for the New York Giants (1948–50) left his position to try to tackle the quarterback. He was successful, and a new strategy was born: linebackers trying to stop the pass at its point of origin. Today it is called blitzing or rushing. Then, it was named after the man who first did it. Red was his nickname (he had red hair) and he was dogging the quarterback. Hence, "Red dogging." Who was he?

A. Red Miller   B. Red Grange
C. Don "Red" Ettinger   C. "Red" Simpson

17. All professional footballs are manufactured in Ohio in what town?

A. Canton   B. Ada
C. Warren   D. Cleveland

18. How many officials must be on the field during a game (not including substitutes)?

A. 5   B. 6
C. 7   D. 8

19. How many of the *original* AFL teams have won Super Bowls?

    A. 4   B. 5
    C. 6   D. 7

20. In 1948 a halfback/tailback/defensive back named Fred Gehrke thought that the solid-colored helmets of his team were dull and ugly. He then decided to change them. After getting permission he took home all of the team's helmets and laboriously hand-painted pro football's first helmet design. It still exists today. What team did he play for?

    A. Los Angeles Rams   B. Minnesota Vikings
    C. Baltimore Colts   D. Green Bay Packers

IN NAME ONLY

The following section is devoted to the unusual combinations of players who, except for sharing the same last names and playing on the same team at the same time, have very little or nothing at all in common. For example, Larry and Robert Woods who played for the Jets in 1974–75.

Below are twenty pairs of first names of sometimes-memorable players from past and present (close of the 1979 season). With them are listed their teams, their positions, and the years they played together.

We did try to avoid focusing on ridiculously obscure players with common names such as Tom and Marvin Johnson who played together for one year with the Green Bay Packers in 1952. But we slipped a few in anyway.

(As an added hint the answers list in reversed alphabetical order.)

1. Jack (DE) and Jim (LB) have been playing for the Los Angeles Rams since 1973.

2. Randy (DT) and Danny (QB/P) have been playing for the Dallas Cowboys since 1976.

3. Mike (T) and John (G/T/C) have been playing for the New Orleans Saints since 1977.

4. Larry (WR) and Chuck (G) played for the Detroit Lions from 1969 through 1974.

5. Charlie (TE) and Ken (DE), also with the Lions, played together from 1972 through 1977.

6. Mike (RB) and Greg (RB) have been playing for the Cleveland Browns since 1976.

7. Preston (RB) and Drew (WR) have been playing for the Dallas Cowboys since 1975.

8. Wayne (T) and Nat (WR) played for the Miami Dolphins from 1974 through 1977.

9. Willie (WR) and Cleo (RB) played for the Cleveland Browns from 1975 through 1976.

10. John (Head Coach) and John (WR) are father and son with the Tampa Bay Buccaneers since 1976.

11. Robert E. (G) and Robert Lee (LB) have been playing for the Denver Broncos since 1978.

12. Tom (LB) and Bernie (DB) have been playing for the Cleveland Browns since 1977.

13. Percy (WR) and Ron (TE) have been playing for the Dallas Cowboys since 1975.

14. J. D. (WR) and David (TE) have been playing for the Detroit Lions since 1976.

15. LeRoy (FB) and Duriel (WR) have been playing for the Miami Dolphins since 1977.

16. Nick (T) and Lou (LB/C) played together for the Brooklyn Dodgers in 1947.

17. Mike (LB) and Tom (DB) played for the Baltimore Colts from 1970 through 1971.

18. Marvin (DB) and Mike (TE) have been playing for the Cincinnati Bengals since 1977.

19. Stan (OG) and Marion (DT/DE/OT) played for the Philadelphia Eagles from 1959 through 1961.

20. Eddie (DB) and Larry (RB) played for the Washington Redskins from 1975 through 1976.

TIME OUT

Sports heroes have long been endorsing non-sports-related products. Joe Namath started a trend for football players by baring all in a panty-hose commercial, and now many football players have mastered the TV ad scene. Whether it be Wheaties or Samsonite, some football player somewhere loves it and wants more than anything else to tell us about it. Apparently, when a football player speaks, we listen.

Match each player with the product he advertises. (There are matches with *all* products listed. A few players have endorsed more than one of the products indicated.)

1. Mercury Morris

2. Lee Roy Jordan

3. Dave Rowe

4. Don Meredith

5. Bob Lilly

6. Frank Gifford

7. Roger Staubach and Drew Pearson

8. Steve Towle

A. "Sports Phone"

B. Subaru

C. Ford Vans

D. Schlitz Natural Light Beer

E. Samsonite Luggage

F. Dry Sack Sherry

G. Happy Days Chewing Tobacco

H. Coca-Cola

9. Pittsburgh Steelers	I. U.S. Commemorative Stamps
10. Fred Dryer and Ken Stabler	J. Swanson's Frozen Dinners
11. O.J. Simpson	K. Skoal Chewing Tobacco
12. Earl Campbell and Walt Garrison	L. Brut Faberge
13. Joe Namath	M. Volkswagen Beetle
14. John Medenhall	N. Lipton Tea
15. Deacon Jones	O. 7-Up
16. Otis Sistrunk	P. Black and Decker Tools
17. Gale Sayers	Q. Pennzoil
18. Richard Todd	R. Miller Lite Beer
19. Dick Butkus	S. Schick
20. Larry Czonka	T. Volkswagen Vans
21. Fran Tarkenton	U. "Dynavit"
22. Pat Haden and Thomas Henderson	V. Timex
23. Nick Buoniconti	W. Johnson's Baby Shampoo
24. "Mean" Joe Greene	X. Hamilton Beach Corn Popper
25. Rocky Blier	Y. Hertz Rent-a-Car

The names of some great and not so great kickers and/or punters have been translated into yet another code here. As before, their teams and the years spent with each team are listed.

1. JLG ZAG
   Oakland Raiders, 1973– .

2. OVH PSDLCLMG
   Detroit Lions, 1978– .

3. WAKSG CQDOP
   Denver Broncos, 1977– .

4. JAPPTDD TJIDTWTM
   New Orleans Saints, 1979– .

5. CLFT XTMMQMZP
   New York Giants, 1974– .

6. DVA "ORT OVT" ZJVEL
   Cleveland Browns, 1946–67.

7. STMMG FQMGLJC
   Atlanta Falcons, 1970.

8. HLJS HVPTDTG
   Philadelphia Eagles, 1970. Houston Oilers, 1971–72.
   Washington Redskins, 1974– .

9. ULO PAHHTJLDD
   Detroit Lions, 1952. Chicago Cardinals, 1953–57. New
   York Giants, 1958–61.

10. OLC NTTC
    Pittsburgh Steelers, 1955.

NAME FIND (DEFENSIVE BACKS)

Find the last names of these defensive backs hidden in the puzzle.

1. Herb ADDERLY

2. Dick ANDERSON

3. Lem BARNEY

4. Mel BLOUNT

5. Bobby BRYANT

6. Mike COBB

7. Neal CRAIG

8. Ken ELLIS

9. Cliff HARRIS

10. Bobby HOWARD

11. Paul KRAUSE

12. Yale LARY

13. Dick LEBEAU

14. Spider LOCKHART

15. Zeke MOORE

16. Brig OWENS

17. Vernon PERRY

18. Doug PLANK

19. Ken RILEY

20. Jake SCOTT

21. Jack TATUM

22. Emmitt THOMAS

23. Emlen TUNNEL

24. Roger WEHRLI

25. Willie WOOD

```
A D D E R L Y E R O O M
L R O N P E R R Y I L J
L A Q U L E B E A U A S
E W B I M T N U O L B C
N O R U K R S T E N O O
N H T N A Y R B C B W T
U A A B S A N U B E R T
T L W E H R L I N A H A
P D I K R A U S E O T P
Q O C R A I G B M I E Z
N O S R E D N A B T O I
L W E L L I S I R R A H
```

FOOTBALL CONNECTIONS

In football, as in most aspects of life, the oddest similarities can be found between what at first inspection seem to be completely unrelated. Take the case of the following three teams: San Francisco 49ers, Denver Broncos, Seattle Seahawks. They are not in the same division or even in the same conference. They have never been owned by the same man or coached by the same man. They might have or may have had a few individual players in common, but for all intents and purposes they are completely dissimilar, right? Wrong. All three teams have starting quarterbacks that are ex-Cowboys: Steve DeBerg, Craig Morton, Jim Zorn. We never said it was easy. However, rest assured, answers to the questions below are somewhat more obvious.

1. Terry Bradshaw, Bart Starr, Chuck Howley.

2. Earl Campbell, John Cappelletti, Archie Griffin, Roger Staubach.

3. Y. A. Tittle, Johnny Unitas, Bert Jones.

4. Green Bay Packers,   New York Jets,
   Pittsburgh Steelers.

5. Dan Devine,   Lou Holtz,   Bill Walsh.

6. Super Bowl IV,   Super Bowl VIII,
   Super Bowl IX,   Super Bowl XI.

7. Otto Graham,   Sid Luckman,   Guy Chamberlain.

8. Bert Bell,   Mike McCormack,   Dick Vermeil.

9. Terry Metcalf,   Anthony Davis,   Tom Cousineau.

10. Alex Wojciechowicz,   Yale Lary,   Greg Landry,
    Billy Sims.

CHALK TALK

The discussion of plays by diagramming them on a blackboard in the classroom is known to football players as a chalk talk. Herein are ten diagrams of different formations and special plays. Each one is followed by a brief explanation and question.

SCRIMMAGE LINE —

○ ○ ○ © ○ ○ ○
　　　　　○ QB

　　　　　○ FB

　　　　　○ HB

　　　　　○ TB

1. The offensive formation shown here was invented in the 1950s by a college coach named Tom Nugent. What is it called?

The two defensive formations shown here are two versions of essentially the same thing. The differences are subtle but important.

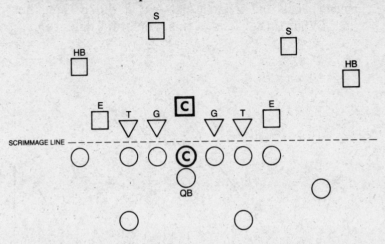

2. This, the earlier of the two, was developed in 1950 by Steve Owen, coach of the New York Giants, to shut down the Cleveland Browns' formidable passing attack. It worked. What is its name?

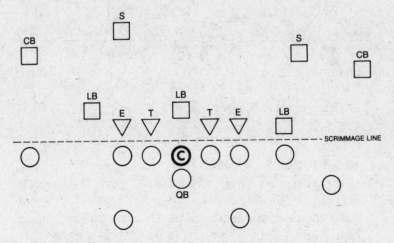

3. This defense was a direct result of the previous forma-

tion. After free substitutions became legal, players no longer had to play offense *and* defense thus creating the possibility of specialized positions: linebackers and cornerbacks and even athletes that did nothing but kick. What is the name of this "separate" defense?

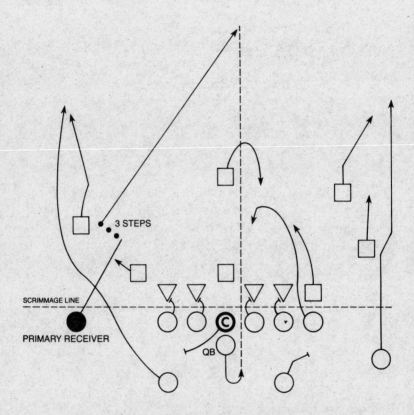

4. From 1949 through 1957 the Los Angeles Rams used this play whenever they wanted to score. The primary receiver, indicated in the diagram, made this bomb pattern one of the most unique (because of his running style) and feared plays in football. Who was the primary receiver?

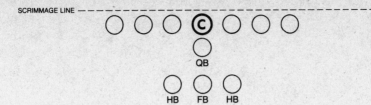

5. This offensive formation was the result of the then-new rule requiring seven men to be on the line of scrimmage when the ball is snapped. What is it called?

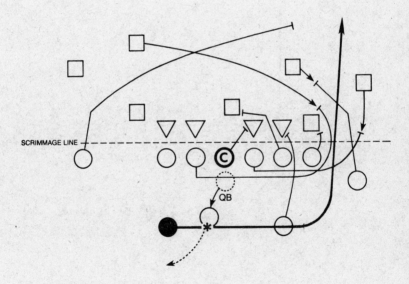

6. This is a diagram of a power sweep utilized by the Chicago Bears from 1965 to 1971. Who would have been the ball carrier (indicated by heavy line) and who would have been the two pulling guards?

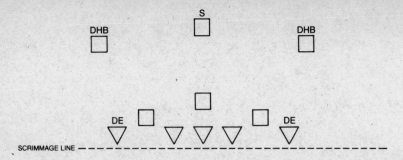

7. At the time, the 1930s, this defense was the most brazen step taken in changing football formations. In order to get more men in the backfield, they reduced the number of men on the line from six to five. What is it?

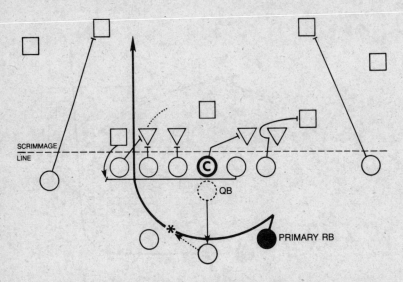

PRIMARY RB

8. This formation has become a trademark of Roger Staubach and the Dallas Cowboys but is actually a revival of a formation created by Red Hickey, coach of the San Francisco 49ers in 1960. The play often begins with the quarterback under the center. Before the snap the quarterback shifts back. Name the formation and the rarely used but startlingly effective play shown

(the primary Dallas running back has usually been Preston Pearson).

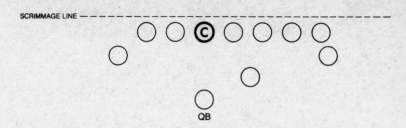

9. Glenn "Pop" Warner developed this innovative offense perhaps as early as 1911 when at Carlisle. This formation laid the foundation for offenses that are still used today. One of them is diagramed next. What did Warner name his offense?

10. Illustrated here are twelve common pass patterns run by wide receivers. Name them.

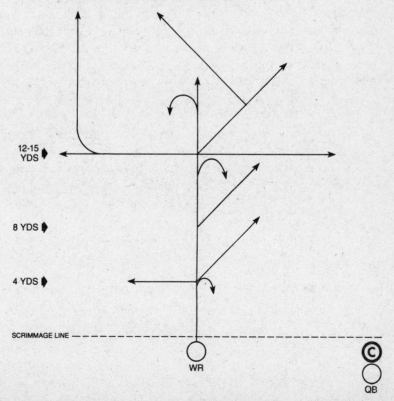

 # FOOTBALL "STARS"

"You gotta be a football hero to get along with the beautiful girls." It also helps if you're a stage, movie or TV star. Over the years many gridiron greats have decided to be both football hero and show biz star. From Frankie Albert to Fred Williamson. From Ed Jones (one line in *Semi Tough*) to guest appearances by Bubba Smith and Garo Yepremian on the television series "The Odd Couple."

The football players below are among the few that have graced the stage or screen, trading yard lines for script lines. Match them with their thespian attempts.

1. Ben Davidson

A. A barroom brawler in *Hooper*.

2. Larry Csonka

B. Starred in a somewhat biographical movie which used his nickname as the title.

3. O. J. Simpson

C. Had a bit part as a naval officer in *Midway*.

4. Alex Karras

D. A vicious, but nice, defensive end for the L.A. Rams in *Heaven Can Wait*.

5. Elroy Hirsch

E. A baseball player in Jim Bouton's short-lived TV series, "Ball Four."

6. Deacon Jones

F. When *One Minute to Play* opened in the Colony Theater on Broadway (his acting debut), he received rave reviews comparing him to Valentino.

7. Jim Brown

G. Shot to pieces in *The Dirty Dozen*, his luck improved when he co-starred in *100 Rifles*, with Raquel Welch.

8. Don Meredith

H. He has been in many TV movies, but his role as Mongo in *Blazing Saddles* was the highlight of his career.

9. Red Grange

I. He has appeared several times on the popular TV series "Police Story."

10. Terry Bradshaw

J. He was a kind-hearted security guard in *The Towering Inferno* and an astronaut in *Capricorn One*.

NAME FIND
(RUNNING BACKS)

Find the last names of these running backs hidden in the puzzle.

1. Ricky BELL
2. Rocky BLIER
3. Cullen BRYANT
4. Dexter BUSSEY
5. Don CALHOUN
6. Ronnie COLEMAN
7. Anthony DAVIS
8. Ike FORTE
9. Clark GAINES
10. Dave HAMPTON
11. Franco HARRIS
12. Calvin HILL
13. Roland HOOKS
14. Jim JENSEN
15. Rick KANE

16. Jim KIICK
17. Horace KING
18. Ron LEE
19. Kevin LONG
20. Herb LUSK
21. Emery MOOREHEAD
22. Tony NATHAN
23. Robert NEWHOUSE
24. Jim OTIS
25. Walter PAYTON
26. Tony REED
27. Gale SAYERS
28. Billy SIMS
29. Wendell TYLER
30. Don WOODS
31. Ricky YOUNG

G	I	K	L	O	C	E	W	B	L	S	H
N	A	C	A	L	H	O	U	N	U	K	A
U	S	I	T	O	I	S	L	S	S	O	M
O	F	I	N	Y	S	H	M	E	K	O	P
Y	O	K	A	E	L	I	O	L	M	H	T
S	R	E	Y	A	S	E	O	W	B	A	O
N	T	N	R	O	K	N	R	E	L	R	N
O	E	A	B	X	G	S	E	I	I	R	A
T	B	L	E	E	D	Z	H	J	E	I	T
Y	E	S	U	O	H	W	E	N	R	S	H
A	L	Y	O	S	I	V	A	D	S	E	A
P	L	W	G	N	I	K	D	E	E	R	N

FOURTH AND LONG

Fourth and long, late in an important game on the down end of a losing score is perhaps the most difficult situation a coach or player can face. The decision of what to do at that moment is often the culmination of many years of participation and observation, taking into account all the little shreds of information gathered through the years. These include both the victories and the mistakes. Even then, though the decision on what to do may be right, a divot in the field, a change in the wind, or some other unpredictable factor can foul things up.

And so, as you browse through the questions within this final section, try to remember all that you have ever seen and heard about the game. The questions are arranged in chronological order. Most of you will have to work through to the 1920s and '30s before the names and teams become familiar, but keep in mind that for the most part the players were all great men, the teams were all great teams, and they are *all* worth remembering.

1. On November 27, 1897, a match between the teams of Latrobe and Greensburg was begun one hour and twenty minutes after its scheduled starting time of three o'clock. The reason for the delay was the pres-

ence of a guard named Core in the Greensburg line. Core was a W&J guard and thereby considered a ringer.

An agreement existed at the time between the two teams that neither side could play any man who was not either in the game on the previous Saturday or among the subs. Latrobe claimed that Core, although on the sidelines the previous Saturday, had not been in uniform and therefore could not be classified a sub. Greensburg, on the other hand, claimed they had the right to use him since he was wearing a Greensburg sweater on the day in question, which designated him a sub. Latrobe insisted that a sweater was not a uniform and therefore he should not be allowed to play.

Both teams bluffed, argued, left the stadium, and returned. Finally a decision was made, the game was played, and Greensburg went home the victors, 6–0. What was the decision made about Core?

2. Playing football indoors is generally considered to be a fairly recent phenomenon. However, quite the contrary is true. 1902 is the date of the first indoor game. The legendary Glenn "Pop" Warner participated at guard. What two teams competed in that game and where was it played?

3. From about 1903 to 1919 the Canton Bulldogs faced their toughest rival regularly at Agathon Field. The betting on games when these two teams met was so violent and corrupt that the bad publicity (among other things) eventually led to the demise of both clubs. What was the name of the Bulldogs' archrivals?

4. A. E. Staley, owner of the Staley Starch Works in Illinois, hired George Halas in 1920 to play for his company baseball team and run his football team. Halas recruited, in that one year, some of football's

finest players. George Halas himself played end, Guy Chamberlain played the other end, George Trafton played center, Jimmy Conzelman was at halfback, Hugh Blacklock at tackle, and Jerry Jones at guard. They finished the year with a 5–1–2 record.

The following year Staley suggested that Halas take the team to Chicago where he could get more exposure and a greater following. Before Halas came to own the team and changed the name to the Chicago Bears in 1922, for that one year (1921) the team retained its original name. What was it?

5. This American Indian tailback, end, and fullback was elected the head of the American Professional Foot Ball Association in September of 1920. That year he was also a player-coach for the Canton Bulldogs. The next year he was the same for the Cleveland Indians and in 1922 and 1923 for the Oorang Indians. With the 1924 season he moved as a player to the Rock Island Independents. At the beginning of the 1925 season he was with the New York Giants, but by the end of the year he had returned to Rock Island. Perhaps for nostalgia, this former Olympian rejoined his old Canton squad in 1926 for just that one season. He rested during the 1927 season and played his final year with the Chicago Cardinals in 1928.

6. In 1921 the Chicago Cardinals started the trend of using an out-of-town training camp during the off-season. Where was the camp located?

7. The (Tampa Bay) Buccaneers were not the first team to be so named. In 1926 a famous road team coached by Tut Imlay and Rick Muller took the name Buccaneers when they represented what city? They finished that single season with a 6–3–1 record.

8. Chief Big Twig played offensive guard, offensive end, and center for the Akron Pros in 1926 and the Buffalo Bison in 1929. What was his slightly more anglicized name?

9. In 1927 a chocolate-covered, peanut-filled candy bar was named after a great athlete of that era. He was the first football player to be so honored. Who was he?

10. In 1927 Earl Pottieger coached his team to an 11–1–1 season. His defense earned the reputation of being the stingiest in all of football. Throughout those thirteen games they allowed only two touchdowns. One on a pass and one on a run. The only team that beat them was the Cleveland Indians who won on two field goals (6–0). What team did this brutal defense play for and which team(s) scored the two touchdowns?

11. On November 28, 1929, in a game between the Chicago Bears and the Chicago Cardinals, this running back set a record that is still unbroken: "Most points scored in a single game."

12. In the 1920s how much did it cost to see the Canton Bulldogs play at Lakeside Park?

13. About fifty years later, in January 1979, pairs of *goal-line* tickets for Super Bowl XIII, between Pittsburgh and Dallas, were selling easily, fifteen minutes before the kick-off, for what outlandish sum?

14. To call this man a living legend would be simply giving him his due.

   For three years, while at the University of Minnesota, he played every position except quarterback and center. In his senior year (1929) only ten men were

named to the All-American Team. He was named both
tackle and fullback. In 1930 he joined the Chicago
Bears. More tales of blinding speed and Herculean
strength are told about this fullback/linebacker and his
eight years straight (and one year in 1943) with the
Bears than any one football player before or since.

In 1936, in Chicago, during a game against
Pittsburgh, two Pirate defensive backs tried to stop
him from reaching the end zone. One suffered a broken
shoulder and the other was knocked unconscious.

Later that evening, on the train bearing back the
defeated Pirate team, the Bear fullback was the topic
of awestruck conversation. Suddenly the train lurched
violently and amid the flying suitcases and football
players was heard the cry: "Run for your lives, men.
It's [Who?]!"

15. The first NFL Championship Game was played in 1933
between two division champs (their leading passers
were Keith Molesworth and Harry Newman) before
17,886 fans. The winners took home a then-incredible
$210.34 (per player) while the losers earned $140.22
(per player). Which two teams battled it out for the
"big money" in Chicago that year and who won?

16. *The Chicago Tribune* sponsored the first Annual College All-Star Game in 1934. For forty-one years the
best of the college players were pitted against pro
football's champions until it was discontinued in 1975
due to lack of viewer interest. The games were, in a
word, boring.

The first game was certainly an undeniable omen.
What pro team met the All-Stars and what was the
memorable score?

17. The advent of World War II wrought many unusual
circumstances. To aid the war effort in 1943 two teams

merged and created a very famous combination franchise. Which were the two teams, and what was the merged franchise called?

18. In 1944 there was another NFL team merger. This combination was less effective, less famous, and plagued with problems. What teams merged for the 1944 season?

19. On December 16, 1945, the Cleveland Rams and the Washington Redskins confronted each other on a frozen field in Cleveland's Municipal Stadium to decide the NFL championship. Accompanying the just barely above zero temperature were gusts of icy wind whipping up to nearly fifty miles per hour.

   Early in the first quarter the Redskins took over possession of the ball after halting a Ram drive on their own 5½-yard line. Their first play resulted in a penalty for intentional grounding (half the distance to the goal-line). The ball was now inside their 3. On the next play Wayne Miller (an end) broke into the secondary wide open. Sammy Baugh dropped back into his own end zone and passed to what should have been a clear touchdown. But as he released the ball a gust of wind came up and blew it right into the crossbar (which was then located on the goal line). The ball bounced back and landed in the end zone. The referee's call that followed essentially decided the game. What was the ruling on that play?

20. "The Million Dollar Backfield" consisted of four great backs: Paul Christman, Pat Harder, Charly Trippi, and Elmer Angsman. Together they led this team to three great seasons (1947–49). What team did they play for?

The battle between the Cleveland Browns and the Los Angeles Rams on December 24, 1950, is often considered to be one of the greatest games ever played. That championship game produced many a hero and goat.

21. What was the name of the running back who scored the game's first touchdown for the Rams, on an 82-yard pass?

22. Who was the Rams' quarterback?

23. Who scored the first touchdown for the Browns, on a 31-yard pass?

24. Who threw the ball to him?

25. The Los Angeles Rams defeated the New York Giants, 23–17 in a 1955 pre-season game that was played in Portland, Oregon. What could possibly be significant about this game?

26. In 1956 the Baltimore Colts needed a quarterback. Their search was long and difficult, but they finally found a promising prospect playing sandlot ball. His name was Johnny Unitas, a virtual unknown who within a single season became the league's leading quarterback. How much did it cost to the Colts to get Unitas to try out?

27. Snow covered the field late in the fourth quarter of a game in 1958 between the Giants and the Cleveland Browns that would determine the possibility of the Giants continuing to the playoffs. The Giants needed to win in order to create a tie in their division with the Browns and therefore force a tie-breaker playoff.

 The score was tied at 10–10. The Giants had the ball, fourth and long on the Cleveland 42. The stadium was getting dark as 63,000 fans watched Charley Connerly (the Giant quarterback) meticulously brush away the snow from where he would place the ball. They waited for the kicker, who just minutes earlier had missed on a 36-yard attempt. Naturally, he kicked the field goal and won the game. Who is he?

28. On August 18, 1962, at 6:30 P.M., the NFL held its first double-header event. Name the four teams that participated. (Hint: It was played in Cleveland Stadium.)

Seventeen minutes and fifty-four seconds into the sudden death period of the 1962 AFL Championship Game a 25-yard field goal ended the two-year reign of the Houston Oilers as the top team in the relatively new league.

29. Which team was responsible for knocking off the Oilers?

30. Who kicked the winning field goal?

31. The San Diego Chargers were a fun team to watch in the '60s. In 1963 not only did they have an exciting passing attack with Lance Alworth, they also possessed a tantalizing backfield with an old quarterback and two quick, talented running backs. Besides being exciting, the Chargers were good! Good enough to beat the Boston Patriots in the 1963 AFL Championship game 51–10.
    Name the three starting members of the Chargers' backfield.

After this team's first game ever in 1966, although they played admirably in losing only 19–14 to the strong Los Angeles Rams, their coach, Norb Hecker, was bitter enough to accuse a recently cut kicker of divulging his game plan to the Rams. But as Rams coach George Allen pointed out, "If we knew what they were going to do, we wouldn't have gone down to the last minute of the game in a position to lose."

32. Name the defeated team.

33. Name the displaced kicker who allegedly squealed.

When the NFL and the AFL merged (under the name of the NFL) two conferences were formed from the existing league. They were called the NFC and the AFC. After thirty-five hours and forty-five minutes of heated argument, the twenty-six team owners, AFL and NFL, compromised on the alignment that exists today—excepting, of course, the then nonexisting Tampa Bay Buccaneers and Seattle Seahawks. According to this compromise, though, three teams that had previously been members of the NFL would join the American Football Conference.

34. Name the three teams and the divisions they entered.

35. Howard Cosell announced the first "Monday Night Football" game on September 21, 1970. What two teams competed in that game? Which team won?

36. With only two seconds left in the game, the New Orleans Saints' Joe Scarpati placed the ball on his own 37-yard line and awaited his team's last, desperate attempt to top the Detroit Lions' 17–16 edge. As those final seconds ticked off the clock that evening (November 8, 1970) Tom Dempsey, the Saint placekicker, made history by breaking Bert Re-chichar's record (56 yards) for the longest field goal ever kicked. The ball traveled an amazing 63 yards. Despite this brilliant performance, however, Tom

Dempsey was traded that year and then three times again during the remainder of his career. Can you recall the four teams he played for after New Orleans?

37. During the 1971 season the Detroit Lions possessed the most powerful running attack in the league. The backfield consisted of Greg Landry at quarterback and which two starting running backs?

38. On December 25, 1971, the Kansas City Chiefs faced the Miami Dolphins in a game to be remembered as the longest game ever played in pro football history (82 minutes and 40 seconds). Obviously, the game went into sudden-death overtime. After a little more than five and a half quarters, Garo Yepremian kicked a field goal, giving the Dolphins a 27–24 victory. Who was the holder for Yepremian?

39. Of what significance was the second game between Kansas City and Oakland during the 1975 season, which the Raiders won 28–20?

In Super Bowl X a blocked punt in the fourth quarter changed the momentum of the game.

40. Name the reserve Steeler running back who blocked the kick.

41. Identify the Dallas punter.

42. Super Bowl X was the scene of the famous "Million Dollar Catch." Who was its receiver and why was his reception so named?

43. The fact that a team has had few season turnovers is supposed to be indicative of a strong club. However,

this team led the league in fewest fumbles (8) in 1977 and still finished with a mediocre 5–9 record.

The Tampa Bay Buccaneers joined the NFL as an expansion team in 1975, but it wasn't until November 11, 1977, the second-to-last game of that season, that they finally won their first game. Previous to that they had lost twenty-six straight.

44. Which team was humiliated in front of its hometown fans by the Buc's?

45. Name the starting quarterback who led the Buc's to this 33–14 trouncing.

46. Accompanying the "just discovered" Buc offense was a defense which sacked the opposing quarterbacks five times and intercepted their passes six times—three for touchdowns, tying an NFL single-game record. Name the three men who returned the three interceptions for touchdowns.

47. Of what significance was the game played between the Kansas City Chiefs and the Cincinnati Bengals (the Bengals won 27–7) on December 4, 1977?

Perhaps the most controversial call of 1977 came during the fourteenth game of the season between the Baltimore Colts and the New England Patriots.

The Colts, who trailed the Patriots at one point during the third quarter 21–3, were moving down the field late in the fourth quarter to destroy New England's 24–23 lead. They had marched from their own one-yard line to within the Patriot's ten when Lydell Mitchell failed to hear Bert Jones' checkoff of the original call at the line of scrimmage. A busted play resulted. Jones was forced to keep the ball himself and was immediately swarmed by Patriot defensemen. Jones fell at the six and the whistle was blown. But, unseen by the referee was the fact that Jones had fumbled and a Patriot linebacker recovered the ball at the ten. The play, though was ruled dead at the six and the Colts retained possession of the ball. They went on to score the winning touchdown. The game ended 30–24.

The more than questionable call resulted in a touchdown that eliminated the Miami Dolphins from the playoffs (even though they had nothing to do with this game).

48. Name the Patriot linebacker who recovered Bert Jones' non-fumble.

49. Who was the referee who, because of his unfortunate positioning, blew the call?

We originally planned to leave you with something relatively simple (something you could answer in a thousand years) but then we thought: Why should we?

50. In 1893 David J. Berry founded the first professional football team. This team, the legendary Greensburg squad, has so far the unmatched and unrivaled distinction of having all of its fourteen members unanimously considered to be professional football's players of the year. Not to detract from the greatness of the feat but merely to indicate that there were extenuating circumstances, one might point out that the second professional football team, the Jeanette squad, was not founded until the following year, 1894.

Name the fourteen original members of the Greensburg team.

END ZONE (ANSWERS)

KICKOFF

Left to right, the players are: Roger Staubach, Franco Harris, Joe Namath. Each won his MVP award while starting for the first time in a Super Bowl; each won his award in a Super Bowl having a number divisible by 3: Namath—III, Staubach—VI, Harris—IX.

WE'RE #1

1. At present there has not been a single Heisman Trophy winner voted in.

2. Charles W. Follis.

3. Eddie Wood.

4. Joe Carr, president from 1921–39.

5. Benny Friedman.

6. Beattie Feathers: Chicago Bears, 1934–37. Brooklyn Dodgers, 1938–39. Green Bay Packers, 1940.

7. Jay Berwanger, a halfback.

8. Eddie LeBaron.

9. Del Shofner: Los Angeles Rams, 1957–60. New York Giants, 1961–67.

   Lifetime stats:

	Receptions	*Yards*
	349	6,470
	Average	*TDs*
	18.5	51

10. Don Meredith. He decided, though, to go to the Cowboys.

11. Los Angeles, New York, Dallas, Denver, Houston, and Minneapolis–St. Paul.

12. Tom Landry.

13. Max McGee of the Green Bay Packers scored on a 37-yard pass from Bart Starr.

14. Don Chandler.

15. Fred Carr, linebacker, Green Bay Packers.

    Mel Renfro, defensive back/punt returner/kick returner, Dallas Cowboys. (He received offensive MVP as a PR/KR.)

16. Larry Brown.

17. Larry Csonka and Jim Kiick.

18. Jim Jodat.

19. Tony Hill

Receptions	Yards	Average	TDs
60	1,062	17.7	10

Drew Pearson

Receptions	Yards	Average	TDs
55	1,026	18.65	8

20. Bob Lilly.

21. Dutch Clark of the Portsmouth Spartans

22. Charlie Evans and the Washington Ambassadors

23. Twenty-eight-year-old journeyman Virgil Carter

NICKNAMES

1. B		14. A	
2. A		15. B	
3. C		16. C	
4. A		17. A	
5. D		18. B	
6. C		19. C	
7. D		20. A	
8. B		21. D	
9. C		22. B	
10. B		23. D	
11. A		24. C	
12. D		25. A	
13. D			

MUDDLE IN THE HUDDLE #1
(CENTERS)

CODE SOLUTION:

A	B	C	D	E	F	G	H	I	J	K	L	M
F	N	J	P	U	S	B	W	O	K	E	Z	C

N	O	P	Q	R	S	T	U	V	W	X	Y	Z
V	X	R	G	I	M	Q	D	Y	A	L	T	H

1. Ray Mansfield
2. Jim Otto
3. Ken Bowman
4. John Fitzgerald
5. Carl Mauck

6. George Karstens
7. Mel Hein
8. Jeff Van Note
9. Dick Szymanski
10. Rich Saul

HOME-FIELD ADVANTAGE

1. Houston Astrodome. Houston Oilers.
   "The Tyler Rose" is Earl Campbell's (RB) nickname. The Astrodome was the first dome built in the U.S. (1965).

2. Shea Stadium. New York Jets.
   The 1964 World's Fair was held in Flushing Meadows, Queens, New York.

3. Schaefer Stadium. New England Patriots.
Schaefer Stadium is located in Foxboro, Mas-
sachusetts between Boston and Providence.

4. Texas Stadium. Dallas Cowboys.
In an effort to retain the outdoor feel of the stadium
and at the same time protect the fans from the
weather, the roof was left partially open, giving it
the appearance of being "unfinished." Texas Stadium
is located in Irving, Texas.

5. Aloha Stadium. Hawaii.
Aloha Stadium has only been used once by professional football, for the '79 season's Pro Bowl. The
location proved to be so popular that it will be used
again for the 1980 season.

6. Tulane Stadium.
Home of the New Orleans Saints until 1975 and the
site of Super Bowl IX.

7. The Kingdome. Seattle Seahawks.
The architects are Naramore, Skilling, and Praeger,
(sorry about that) who completed the dome in 1976.

8. Orange Bowl. Miami Dolphins.
Super Bowls II, III, V, X, and XIII were played in
the Orange Bowl. The Dolphins went seventeen
games undefeated, including the Super Bowl played
in 1973.

9. Meadowlands Complex's Giants Stadium. The
Giants.
The water table in the Meadowlands (New Jersey)
is only just below the surface, meaning that the
stadium was literally built in a swamp.

10. Soldier Field. Chicago Bears.
    Soldier Field houses an auto racetrack and is
    adorned with a colonnade.

11. Metropolitan Stadium. Minnesota Vikings.
    In Metropolitan Stadium, because of the placement
    of the field in relation to the stands, it is impossible
    to have teams on opposite sidelines.
    Roger Staubach threw an amazing 50-yard despera-
    tion "Hail Mary" pass to Drew Pearson in the closing
    minutes of their 1975 playoff game with Minnesota
    to win it 17–14.

12. Rich Stadium. Buffalo Bills.
    The "Electric Company" is the nickname of the Bills'
    offensive line.
    "The Juice" (O. J. Simpson) made Rich Stadium his
    first professional home.

13. Atlanta–Fulton County Stadium. Atlanta Falcons.
    O. J. Simpson played his last professional game
    here. He ran twice: once for 2 yards and the last for
    10.
    Tim Mazzetti was a bartender in Philadelphia when
    he decided in 1978 that he could do better than the
    kicker in Atlanta at the time. He tried out. He made
    it and is still playing.

14. Philadelphia Veterans Stadium. Philadelphia Eagles.
    Joe Brown erected a series of huge bronze statues
    of football players in front of the stadium.
    Spectrum is the name of the famous multipurpose
    sports complex next door to Veterans Stadium.

15. R.F.K. Memorial Stadium. Washington Redskins.
    The stadium, just over Capitol Hill, housed the
    "Over the Hill" gang (Redskins).

16. Arrowhead Stadium. Kansas City Chiefs.
In 1963, Lamar Hunt's Dallas Texans moved to Kansas City and became the Kansas City Chiefs.

17. Mile High Stadium. Denver Broncos.
1,760 yards = 1 mile. (Cute, huh?)
Orange Crush was the nickname of the Broncos' defense until the soda company of the same name brought a lawsuit against the team and demanded that the name not be used.

18. Taft Riverfront Stadium. Cincinnati Bengals.
Paul Brown's second team: the Bengals play in Riverfront Stadium, so named because it faces the Ohio River.

19. Three Rivers Stadium. Pittsburgh Steelers.
The Steelers won Super Bowls IX, X, XIII, and XIV. The "Terrible Towel" is a yellow and black towel bought by Steeler fans and waved at the stadium to cheer on their team.

20. Candlestick Park. San Francisco 49ers.
Bill Walsh is the 49ers' head coach and general manager. The 49ers play just off San Francisco Bay.

21. Busch Memorial Stadium. St. Louis Cardinals.
A common television view makes Busch Stadium appear to be located under the Saint Louis Arch. And it's Busch as in Anheuser-Busch, the brewers of Budweiser beer.

22. Oakland–Alameda County Coliseum. Oakland Raiders.
Al Davis' (GM) Raiders play in the stadium that was built primarily for the Oakland A's (Athletics) baseball team.

23. **Tampa Stadium. Tampa Bay Buccaneers.**
Before the Florida expansion team could play in Tampa, the existing stadium had to be enlarged from 46,000 (when it opened in 1967) to 77,000 when it reopened in 1976.

24. **Pontiac Silverdome. Detroit Lions.**
The Pontiac Silverdome has an inflatable roof attached to a network of cables. It is held up by electric fans that create internal air pressure.

25. **Louisiana Superdome. New Orleans Saints.**

26. **Los Angeles Memorial Coliseum.**
Site of the 1964 Olympics. The Rams moved from the Coliseum to Anaheim in 1980.

27. **The Polo Grounds. New York**
Both the Giants and the New York Titans played at the Polo Grounds.

28. **Lambeau field. Green Bay Packers.**
One of Green Bay's two stadiums (the only team that has two stadiums): Lambeau Field was named after one of their first coaches, Curly Lambeau. Their other stadium is Milwaukee County Stadium.

PLAYER IDENTIFICATIONS
FIRST AND TEN

1. Bob Hayes   21. Jack Lambert

2. Jerry Sherk   22. John Medenhall

3. Franco Harris   23. Tony Dorsett

4. Joe Namath

5. Tom Banks

6. Mark Moseley

7. Doug Williams

8. Steve Grogan

9. Ed Budde and his son, Brad.

10. Chris Bahr

11. Matt Bahr

12. Tommy Kramer

13. Darryl Stingley

14. George Blanda

15. Delvin Williams

16. O. J. Anderson

17. James Larnell Harris

18. Rick Upchurch

19. Wilbert Montgomery

20. Wesley Walker

24. Chuck Foreman

25. J. V. Cain

26. Jim Otto

27. Dave Dalby

28. Wendell Tyler

29. Ken Houston

30. Jim Zorn

31. Lyle Alzado

32. Mel Gray

33. Jack Thompson

34. Terry Bradshaw

35. Vince Ferragamo

36. Matt Robinson

37. Doug Kotar

38. Billy Kilmer

39. Conrad Dobler

40. Roger Staubach

PLAYER IDENTIFICATIONS
SECOND AND EIGHT

1. Chuck Bednarik
2. George Kunz
3. Dave Green
4. Manu Tuiasosopo
5. Walt Garrison
6. Norm Snead
7. Vernon Perry
8. Ed Garvey
9. Deacon Jones
10. Jim Brown
11. Alex Karras (Lions), Paul Hornung (Packers)
12. Gary Fencik and Doug Plank
13. Mike Livingston
14. Chuck Muncie and Tony Galbreath
15. Jim Braxton
16. Jim Marshall

21. Danny Abramowicz
22. Tom Mack
23. Gary Danielson
24. Norm Van Brocklin
25. Dave Jennings
26. Bob Grupp
27. Wilson Whitley, Eddie Edwards, Ross Browner, Gary Burley
28. Raymond Berry
29. Dave Pear
30. Garo Yepremian (the veteran) and Uwe Von Schaman
31. Jerry Butler
32. Joe Pisarcik
33. Ahmad Rashad
34. Earl Morral
35. Leroy Kelly
36. Ken MacAfee

17. Lenny Moore

18. Abdul Salaam

19. Jackie Smith

20. Harold Carmichael

37. Joe Washington

38. Jim Langer

39. Neil O'Donoghue

40. Preston Pearson

PLAYER IDENTIFICATIONS
THIRD AND THIRTEEN

1. Randy Vataha

2. Don Woods. In 1974 he rushed for 1,162 yards.

3. Bobby Douglass

4. Larry Wilson

5. Paul Coffman

6. Dick "Night Train" Lane

7. Tommy Nobis

8. Clint Longley

9. Dave Grayson

10. Jack Rudnay

11. Cecil Turner

12. Bert Bell

13. Dave Hampton

14. Bill Willis

15. Rick Engles

16. Horst Muhlmann

17. Gale Sayers

18. Kermit Alexander

19. Scott Hunter

20. Jerry Tubbs

NAME FIND (COACHES)

```
N  A  B  A  S  Y  K  N  A  B  W  E
E  Z  O  T  R  V  V  H  C  E  L  I
P  A  R  D  E  E  S  I  X  N  H  S
K  A  N  C  N  L  N  E  W  O  A  S
M  A  I  I  A  O  N  O  L  L  N  T
L  R  V  W  E  M  R  T  A  T  N  K
N  E  L  L  A  B  Z  H  I  A  O  R
D  B  A  C  L  A  R  K  R  S  R  E
R  E  P  T  G  R  E  G  G  A  B  L
N  O  M  A  D  D  E  N  T  P  I  L
A  W  I  G  G  I  N  S  E  L  G  I
T  A  D  O  R  B  I  H  C  R  A  M
```

CODE SOLUTION:

A	B	C	D	E	F	G	H	I	J	K	L	M
R	O	L	M	P	A	V	U	Q	N	J	K	B

N	O	P	Q	R	S	T	U	V	W	X	Y	Z
G	Z	C	W	Y	I	D	S	F	E	T	X	H

1. Fred Dryer
2. Bob Lilly
3. Deacon Jones
4. "Mean" Joe Greene
5. Louie Kelcher
6. Steve Niehaus
7. Andy Robustelli
8. LeRoy Selmon
9. Gino Marchetti
10. Ernie Stautner

RAINBOWS TO SIX

(Statistics for currently active players are for all games up to the Fall 1980 season.)

1. I

Johnny Unitas
Baltimore Colts, 1956–72. San Diego Chargers, 1973.

Attempts	Completions	Percentage
5,186	2,830	54.57

Yards	TDs	Interceptions
40,239	290	253

Jimmy Orr
Pittsburgh Steelers, 1958–60.
Baltimore Colts, 1961–70.

Receptions	Yards	Average	TDs
400	7,914	19.79	66

2. J

Roger Staubach
Dallas Cowboys, 1969–80.

Attempts	Completions	Percentage
2,958	1,685	57.2

Yards	TDs	Interceptions
22,700	153	109

Drew Pearson
Dallas Cowboys, 1973–   .

Receptions	Yards	Average	TDs
366	5,723	17.03	33

3. F

Francis Tarkenton
Minnesota Vikings, 1961–66.
New York Giants, 1967-71. Vikings, 1972–78.

Attempts	Completions	Percentage
6,467	3,687	58.49

Yards	TDs	Interceptions
47,003	317	250

Sammie White
Minnesota Vikings, 1976–   .

Receptions	Yards	Average	TDs
187	3,122	16.69	32

4. B
Bart Starr
Green Bay Packers, 1956–71.

Attempts	Completions	Percentage
3,149	1,808	57.42

Yards	TDs	Interceptions
24,718	152	138

Boyd Dowler
Green Bay Packers, 1959–69.
Washington Redskins, 1971.

Receptions	Yards	Average	TDs
474	7,270	15.34	40

5. T
Len Dawson
Pittsburgh Steelers, 1957–59.
Cleveland Browns, 1960–61. Dallas Texans, 1962.
Kansas City Chiefs, 1963–75.

Attempts	Completions	Percentage
3,741	2,136	57.1

Yards	TDs	Interceptions
28,711	239	183

Otis Taylor
Kansas City Chiefs, 1965–75.

Receptions	Yards	Average	TDs
410	7,306	17.82	57

6. S
Terry Bradshaw
Pittsburgh Steelers, 1970–   .

Attempts	Completions	Percentage
2,859	1,474	54.0

Yards	TDs	Interceptions
19,118	147	163

Lynn Swann
Pittsburgh Steelers, 1974– .

Receptions	Yards	Average	TDs
240	3,982	16.59	39

7. M
Sonny Jurgensen
Philadelphia Eagles, 1957–63.
Washington Redskins, 1964–74.

Attempts	Completions	Percentage
4,262	2,433	57.09

Yards	TDs	Interceptions
32,224	255	189

Pete Retzlaff
Philadelphia Eagles, 1956–66.

Receptions	Yards	Average	TDs
452	7,412	16.40	47

8. L
Ken Stabler
Oakland Raiders, 1970–79.
Traded to Houston Oilers in 1980.

Attempts	Completions	Percentage
2,481	1,486	59.9

Yards	TDs	Interceptions
19,078	150	143

Fred Biletnikoff
Oakland Raiders, 1965–79.

Receptions	Yards	Average	TDs
589	8,974	15.31	76

9. A
Joe Namath
New York Jets, 1965–76. Los Angeles Rams, 1977.

Attempts	Completions	Percentage
3,762	1,886	50.13

Yards	TDs	Interceptions
27,663	173	220

Don Maynard
New York Giants, 1958. New York Jets, 1960–72.
St. Louis Cardinals, 1973.

Receptions	Yards	Average	TDs
633	11,834	18.70	88

10. O
Ken Anderson
Cincinnati Bengals, 1971–   .

Attempts	Completions	Percentage
2,785	1,570	55.65

Yards	TDs	Interceptions
20,030	101	125

Isaac Curtis
Cincinnati Bengals, 1973–   .

Receptions	Yards	Average	TDs
249	4,856	19.50	45

11. **H**
John Hadl
San Diego Chargers, 1962–72.
Los Angeles Rams, 1973–74.
Green Bay Packers, 1974–75.
Houston Oilers, 1976–78.

Attempts	Completions	Percentage
4,688	2,362	50.41

Yards	TDs	Interceptions
33,503	244	268

Lance Alworth
San Diego Chargers, 1962–70.
Dallas Cowboys, 1971–72.

Receptions	Yards	Average	TDs
542	10,267	19.94	85

12. **K**
Norm Van Brocklin
Los Angeles Rams, 1949–57.
Philadelphia Eagles, 1958–60.

Attempts	Completions	Percentage
2,611	1,400	53.63

Yards	TDs	Interceptions
21,140	149	161

Elroy Hirsch
Chicago Rockets, 1946–48.
Los Angeles Rams, 1949–57.

Receptions	Yards	Average	TDs
387	7,029	18.16	60

13. **R**
    Dan Fouts
    San Diego Chargers, 1973–   .

Attempts	Completions	Percentage
2,234	1,181	59.45

Yards	TDs	Interceptions
14,739	82	101

    John Jefferson
    San Diego Chargers, 1978–   .

Receptions	Yards	Average	TDs
117	2,091	17.87	23

14. **N**
    Craig Morton
    Dallas Cowboys, 1965–74.
    New York Giants, 1974–76.
    Denver Broncos, 1977–   .

Attempts	Completions	Percentage
3,085	1,626	54.27

Yards	TDs	Interceptions
22,370	150	157

    Haven Moses
    Buffalo Bills, 1968–72. Denver Broncos, 1972–   .

Receptions	Yards	Average	TDs
412	7,256	17.61	52

15. **E**
    Phil Simms
    New York Giants, 1979–   .

Attempts	Completions	Percentage
265	135	50.6

Yards	TDs	Interceptions
1,743	13	14

Ernest Gray
New York Giants, 1979– .

Receptions	Yards	Average	TDs
28	537	19.2	4

16. Q
Bob Griese
Miami Dolphins, 1967– .

Attempts	Completions	Percentage
3,329	1,865	57.97

Yards	TDs	Interceptions
24,302	186	168

Paul Warfield
Cleveland Browns, 1964–69. Miami Dolphins, 1970–74.
WFL, 1975. Cleveland Browns, 1976–77.

Receptions	Yards	Average	TDs
427	8,565	20.06	85

17. G
Dan Pastorini
Houston Oilers, 1971–79.
Traded to Oakland Raiders, 1980.

Attempts	Completions	Percentage
2,768	1,426	51.49

Yards	TDs	Interceptions
16,864	96	176

Ken Burrough
New Orleans Saints, 1970. Houston Oilers, 1971–

Receptions	Yards	Average	TDs
377	6,343	16.82	42

18. P
Otto Graham
Cleveland Browns, 1946–55.

Attempts	Completions	Percentage
2,626	1,464	55.75

Yards	TDs	Interceptions
23,594	174	135

Dante Lavelli
Cleveland Browns, 1946–56.

Receptions	Yards	Average	TDs
376	6,488	16.81	62

Mac Speedeie
Cleveland Browns, 1946–52. CFL 1953.

Receptions	Yards	Average	TDs
349	5,602	16.05	33

19. C
Y. A. Tittle
Baltimore Colts, 1948–50.
San Francisco 49ers, 1951–60.
New York Giants, 1961–64.

Attempts	Completions	Percentage
2,960	1,627	54.97

Yards	TDs	Interceptions
21,937	142	177

Hugh McElhenny
San Francisco 49ers, 1952–60.
Minnesota Vikings, 1961–62.
New York Giants, 1963. Detroit Lions, 1964.

Receptions	Yards	Average	TDs
264	3,247	12.30	20

20. D
Jim Zorn
Seattle Seahawks, 1976–   .

Attempts	Completions	Percentage
1,638	845	53.2

Yards	TDs	Interceptions
11,204	63	84

Steve Largent
Seattle Seahawks, 1976–

Receptions	Yards	Average	TDs
224	3,753	16.75	31

NAME FIND (LINEBACKERS)

H	S	N	R	U	S	S	E	L	L	E	B
K	E	S	U	D	Y	E	G	R	E	B	U
H	A	N	B	U	R	G	E	R	W	B	O
K	A	J	D	I	C	U	R	T	I	S	N
C	D	R	C	E	T	I	H	W	S	N	I
B	H	C	T	A	R	N	O	B	I	S	C
R	U	D	C	A	R	S	O	N	E	U	O
L	R	F	N	A	D	R	O	J	M	K	N
S	I	F	F	O	M	U	A	N	O	T	T
Y	E	L	W	O	H	U	U	M	N	U	I
D	L	R	E	I	N	A	L	E	L	B	Y
B	R	A	Z	I	L	E	C	L	A	I	R

SCRIMMAGED LINES

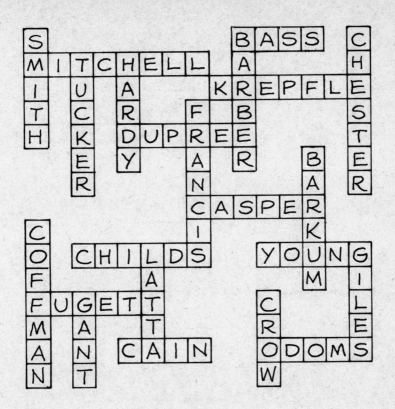

BETWEEN THE HASH MARKS

1. A

2. D

3. B

4. D

11. B

12. A

13. B

14. D

5. C	15. A
6. B	16. C
7. A	17. B
8. A	18. C
9. C	19. A. Jets III, Chiefs IV, Dolphins VII and VIII, Raiders XI.
10. C	20. A

IN NAME ONLY

1. Youngblood	11. Jackson
2. White	12. Jackson
3. Watson	13. Howard
4. Walton	14. Hill
5. Sanders	15. Harris
6. Pruitt	16. Daukas
7. Pearson	17. Curtis
8. Moore	18. Cobb
9. Miller	19. Campbell
10. McKay	20. Brown

1. B

2. M

3. I

4. N

5. P

6. F

7. T

8. G

9. E

10. Q

11. Y

12. K

13. X and L

14. A

15. R

16. V

17. U

18. L

19. C and R

20. S

21. W

22. O

23. D

24. J and H

25. J

MUDDLE IN THE HUDDLE #3
(KICKERS)

CODE SOLUTION:

A	B	C	D	E	F	G	H	I	J	K	L	M
U	F	D	L	Z	V	Y	M	X	R	C	A	N

```
N  O  P  Q  R  S  T  U  V  W  X  Y  Z
W  T  S  I  H  K  E  P  O  B  J  Q  G
```

1. Ray Guy

2. Tom Skladany

3. Bucky Dilts

4. Russel Erxleben

5. Dave Jennings

6. Lou "The Toe" Groza

7. Kenny Vinyard

8. Mark Moseley

9. Pat Summerall

10. Tad Weed

NAME FIND (DEFENSIVE BACKS)

```
A  D  D  E  R  L  Y  E  R  O  O  M
L  R  O  N  P  E  R  R  Y  I  L  J
L  A  Q  U  L  E  B  E  A  U  A  S
E  W  B  I  M  T  N  U  O  L  B  C
N  O  R  U  K  R  S  T  E  N  O  O
N  H  T  N  A  Y  R  B  C  B  W  T
U  A  A  B  S  A  N  U  B  E  R  T
T  L  W  E  H  R  L  I  N  A  H  A
P  D  I  K  R  A  U  S  E  O  T  P
Q  O  C  R  A  I  G  B  M  I  E  Z
N  O  S  R  E  D  N  A  B  T  O  I
L  W  E  L  L  I  S  I  R  R  A  H
```

FOOTBALL CONNECTIONS

1. All three were Super Bowl MVPs.
   Bradshaw (Steelers) XIII and XIV.
   Starr (Packers) I and II.
   Howley (Cowboys) V.

2. All were Heisman Trophy winners.
   Campbell (Texas University) 1978.
   Cappelletti (Penn State University) 1973.
   Griffin (Ohio State University) 1975.
   Roger Staubach (Naval Academy) 1963.

3. All were quarterbacks for the Baltimore Colts.
   Tittle quarterbacked the Colts in 1948–50.
   Unitas quarterbacked the Colts in 1956–72.
   Jones has been quarterbacking the Colts since 1973.

4. The only three teams that have perfect records in the Super Bowl.
   Green Bay is two for two. Super Bowls I and II.
   New York is one for one. Super Bowl III.
   Pittsburgh is four for four. Super Bowls IX, X, XIII, and XIV.

5. All have coached college and pro football.
   Devine coached the University of Missouri, then the Green Bay Packers, 1971–74.
   Holtz coached North Carolina State University, then the Jets in 1976.
   Walsh coached Stanford University, then the 49ers from 1979–   .

6. All Super Bowls in which Minnesota participated (and were subsequently beaten by the Chiefs, Dolphins, Steelers, and Raiders).

7. All were inducted into the Football Hall of Fame in 1965.

Graham, QB: Cleveland Browns, 1946–55, Washington Redskins head coach, 1966–68.

Luckman, QB/DB/HB: Chicago Bears, 1939–50.

Chamberlain, E/TB/Player-Coach: Decatur Staleys, 1920. Chicago Bears, 1921. Canton Bulldogs, 1922–23. Cleveland Browns, 1924. Frankford Yellow Jackets, 1925–26. Chicago Cardinals, 1927.

8. All were or are coaches of the Philadelphia Eagles.
   Bell was head coach from 1936–40.
   McCormack was head coach from 1973–75.
   Vermeil has been head coach since 1976.

9. All defected to the CFL.
   Metcalf left the St. Louis Cardinals in 1977.
   Davis left the Tampa Bay Buccaneers in 1977.
   Cousineau was drafted by the Bills and then left before playing a single game in 1979.

10. All were first-round draft choices for the Detroit Lions.
    Wojciechowicz was drafted in 1938 as a center and linebacker.
    Lary was drafted in 1952 as a defensive back and a punter.
    Landry was drafted in 1968 as a quarterback.
    Sims was drafted in 1980 as a running back.

CHALK TALK

1. The "I" formation. It gets its name from the shape the backfield resembles.

2. The "Umbrella" defense.

3. The 4–3 defense (four linemen, three linebackers).

4. Elroy Hirsch.

5. The "T" formation (the shape without the front line) or the "Fullhouse."

6. Gale Sayers, of course, is the running back.
   George Seals is the left guard making the block on the safety.
   Jim Cadile, the right guard, is making the block on the cornerback.

7. The 5–3 defense (five linemen, three linebackers).

8. The "Shotgun," out of which is run the "Shovel Pass."

9. The "Double Wing" (two split flanker backs called wingbacks).

10.

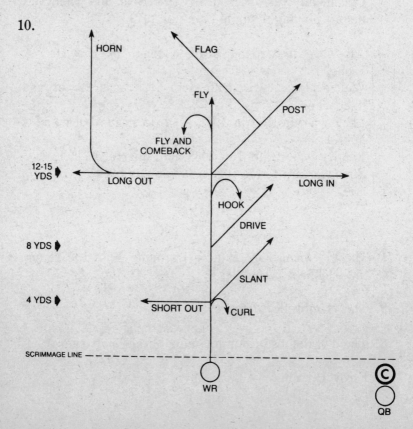

FOOTBALL "STARS"

1. E 3. J 5. B (The movie was 7. G 9. F
           Crazylegs.)

2. C 4. H 6. D 8. I 10. A

NAME FIND (RUNNING BACKS)

```
G  I  K  L  O  C  E  W  B  L  S  H
N  A  C  A  L  H  O  U  N  U  K  A
U  S  I  T  O  I  S  L  S  S  O  M
O  F  I  N  Y  S  H  M  E  K  O  P
Y  O  K  A  E  L  I  O  L  M  H  T
S  R  E  Y  A  S  E  O  W  B  A  O
N  T  N  R  O  K  N  R  E  L  R  N
O  E  Á  B  X  G  S  E  I  I  R  A
T  B  L  E  E  D  Z  H  J  E  I  T
Y  E  S  U  O  H  W  E  N  R  S  H
A  L  Y  O  S  I  V  A  D  S  E  A
P  L  W  G  N  I  K  D  E  E  R  N
```

1. Latrobe won the argument. Core did not play.

2. The Philadelphia Nationals lost to Syracuse (Glenn Warner's team) 6–0, in the original Madison Square Garden.

3. The Massilon Tigers.

4. The Decatur Staleys 1920
   The Chicago Staleys 1921.
   The Chicago Bears 1922–   .

5. Jim Thorpe.

6. Where else but Coldwater, Michigan?

7. Los Angeles.

8. Nat McCombs.

9. Red Grange. The bar's full name is "Shotwell's Red Grange Candy Bar."

10. The New York Giants, believe it or not, had the toughest defense on record, with the Chicago Bears and the Chicago Cardinals scoring the only touchdowns against them. They were both defeated—13–7 and 28–7, respectively.

11. Ernie Nevors. He scored 40 points: 6 touchdowns and 4 PATs.

12. One dollar plus ten cents tax.

13. Approximately $500.

14. Bronko Nagurski.

15. The Chicago Bears played the New York Giants and won 23–21. The winners of the 1979 Pro Bowl, a relatively unimportant game, took home $18,000 apiece.

16. The Chicago Bears confronted the All-Stars and played a scoreless game.

17. The Philadelphia Eagles merged with the Pittsburgh Steelers and became known as the Phil-Pitt Steagles. The merger was dissolved at the end of the 1943 season with a 5–4–1 record.

18. The St. Louis Cardinals combined talent with Pittsburgh to form the Card-Pitt squad. Their final record was 0–10–0.

19. The play was ruled a safety. The Redskins lost 15–16. Twenty-seven days later at the next rules committee meeting George Marshall (the Redskins' owner) had that rule amended.

20. The Chicago Cardinals.

21. Although overshadowed by the other Los Angeles receivers (Elroy Hirsch, Tom Fears, and running back Verda Smith), Glenn Davis did step into the limelight on the game's first play from scrimmage.

22. Bob Waterfield, a kicker who shared season's quarterbacking duties with Norm Van Brocklin (broken ribs).

23. Dub Jones, father of Baltimore's Bert Jones.

24. Otto Graham.

25. It was the first "sudden-death" game ever played in pro ball.

26. Eighty cents—for a phone call.

27. Pat Summerall.

28. The Cleveland Browns vs. the Pittsburgh Steelers. The Detroit Lions vs. the Dallas Cowboys.

29. Dallas Texans.

30. Tommy Brooker.

31. Tobin Rote, quarterback. Paul Lowe, running back. Keith Lincoln, running back.

32. The Atlanta Falcons.

33. Bill Jencks.

34. The Baltimore Colts joined the AFC East (then called Division II) and the Cleveland Browns and the Pittsburgh Steelers joined the AFC Central (then called Division I).

35. The Cleveland Browns beat the New York Jets 31–21.

36. New Orleans Saints (1969–70),
    Philadelphia Eagles (1971–74),
    Los Angeles Rams (1975–76),
    Houston Oilers (1977),
    Buffalo Bills (1978).

37. In his second pro year, Heisman Trophy winner
    Steve Owens finished second in the NFC in total
    yards gained on the ground:

Carries	Yards	Average	TDs
246	1,035	4.2	8

He was more than ably assisted by Altie Taylor:

Carries	Yards	Average	TDs
174	736	4.2	4

38. Wide receiver Karl Noonan.

39. George Blanda topped 2,000 career points.

40. Reggie Harrison.

41. Mitch Hoopes.

42. Percy Howard of the Dallas Cowboys caught a
    thirty-four-yard pass from Roger Staubach in the
    closing minutes of the fourth quarter that made the
    score 17–21 in favor of the Steelers. Although the
    catch did not win the game for the Cowboys it did
    beat the sizable seven-point spread. The money ac-

quired by the Dallas bettors, incidentally, exceeded the million mark several times.

43. The San Francisco 49ers.

44. The New Orleans Saints were beaten in the Louisiana Superdome. Their coach, Hank Stram, later claimed that he burned the game films.

45. Gary Huff completed 7 of 9 passes for 96 yards.

46. Mike Washington, quarterback, returned 45 yards. Richard Wood, linebacker, returned 10 yards. Greg Johnson, defensive end, intercepted while in the end zone.

47. It was the 5,000th game recorded in NFL history.

48. Sam Hunt.

49. Fred Silva.

50. Morrison Barclay, W. C. L. Bayne, Charles Copeland, Richard Coulter, John Cribbs, Tom Donohue, Lawson Fiscus, Leo Furtwangler, Coach Lloyd Huff, Charles Jamison, Tom Jamison, Ed Mechling, Bill Theurer, and Joseph Wentin.